T0159176

THE DATING GAME FOR THE SENIOR GENTLEMAN USING DATING SITES

DR. FERRIS EUGENE MERHISH

authorHOUSE®

AuthorHouse™
1663 Liberty Drive
Bloomington, IN 47403
www.authorhouse.com
Phone: 1 (800) 839-8640

Published by AuthorHouse   02/13/2019

ISBN: 978-1-5462-7705-7 (sc)
ISBN: 978-1-5462-7706-4 (hc)
ISBN: 978-1-5462-7711-8 (e)

Library of Congress Control Number: 2019900756

Print information available on the last page.

This book is printed on acid-free paper.

For Bobbie

CONTENTS

THIS BOOK WAS inspired by my late wife, Bobbie. We were together for nearly twenty-three years, and she was a surprising blessing. My first marriage had ended in divorce, and Bobbie not only brought love and romance back into my life, but she truly was instrumental in helping me to recover from a difficult situation—a financial disaster because of my divorce and the untimely collapse my career.

Throughout our marriage, she was attractive, hardworking, independent, fair, loving, and supportive. Even on her last day with us, she unselfishly tried to assist her younger sister with her loss of her husband and major financial and medical issues. She even unselfishly worked toward helping me with my life after she was gone. She was a very supportive and loving mother; she loved animals, and we even raised Alpacas together.

I have found it extremely difficult to function without her, but I hope that someday I will find another woman to unselfishly share her life with me and not give up on me through times of illness, through the good and the bad times.

After I met Bobbie, there was never a moment when I looked back. Our time together was wonderful, and I looked forward to a long and fruitful, loving life with her. When I lost her to cancer, it broke my heart. I didn't realize it would hurt so much, and it brings tears to my eyes even now.

CHAPTER 1

THERE ARE MANY reasons why someone might seek help in finding a mate. If you are divorced, widowed, or single, you might want to try one of many dating sites. The goal of this book is not to suggest which site is best—everyone has a different opinion; this is why I drive a Ford F-150, and you drive a VW—but I will suggest several of the issues and problems you may face on these sites.

Many dating sites seem to have fewer male participants than female. I won't address the quality of these male participants; as with beauty, this is in the eye of the beholder, and the same quality must be determined by the male participants also. I will present my male view as it relates to the challenges, disappointments, and frustrations you might go through when trying to find the lady of your choice—your companion, girlfriend, lover, friend, pal, or whatever you are looking for. You may have tried hanging out at a bar, but this generally is not a successful undertaking; it wasn't for me, even in my younger days. That said, however, I *did* meet my first wife at a little dance bar in a bowling alley in Cupertino, California.

Oh yes, I do want to touch on this too. Someplace way back in my studies, I can remember a particular fact—you can believe it or not, but I can see a lot of logic behind the statement. Very simply, there are about one hundred women for every available man in the current world. Now, the following is my opinion, so you can take or leave my advice, but here it is: women need to look at their assets and do their best to improve them, but you guys need to put some shine on your apple too.

How did I arrive at these statistics? First of all, discounting illness, we guys don't tend to live as long as women—something like eight years shorter on average. Second, from the beginning of time until today, the reality is that more men are engaged in active combat in the military than women. And here is something else to think about: often, among those men who not accepted into service, many are broken and worn out. I don't want to make anyone mad, but there are a lot of leftovers. I wasn't in a war, but I served in the navy, AFR, National Guard, and more. And I was blown down a flight deck, so I have hearing loss. I am not a perfect candidate either.

We guys often polish our cars, put a lot chrome on them, and make sure there's something a little more special under the hood. Well, your car is not any more special than you are; you need to do the same for yourself. Buy a new shirt; shine your shoes.

Now, gentlemen, you're not going to get off this easy. Sure, you are in short supply, but you can make yourself a better catch. Here is an easy task for you: go out and watch the wildlife. I believe it is the male black widow spider who puts on a little show for his next mate, and if she likes him, she does eat him, but so what? He got his gal, didn't he?

All kidding aside, most of the male species have brighter colors or put on some kind of show for that new mate. So what can you do? Well, let me see—how about stop chewing, have your clothing pressed, get a haircut, too, maybe. Personally I would want you to take a bath more than once a week, and if it was my opinion, I wouldn't want to kiss you either if you don't shave once in a while. One thing I got from the navy: in my day, we showered every day, changed our underwear—and our outerwear too—and shined our shoes!

Now, here is a novel thought. I am going to share this little secret with you. I don't do this all the time, but very often, when I take a gal out on a date, even when meeting her for the first time, I buy her flowers. This costs me anywhere from $5.95 to $20. I have been known to take a lady flowers every day we go out. I have been dating a nice woman for over a month now, and nearly every time I see her, I give her flowers. About a year ago, I did the same thing with someone else, and the gal said to me, "Are you trying to score with me?" And I said yes! What is this going to cost you—the price of a couple of beers? Sure, but you will both benefit. (You do know that beer puts on weight, right?)

I am seventy-eight years old, though women and others have often said I look sixty-five. I am tall—six foot three—I have a most of my own hair and most of my own teeth too (none of them comes out at night, but some are manufactured).

I have a young man who works for me part-time, helping me with work around my house, installing lights, and also some security cameras. He is in his fifties, around my daughter's age. One thing that kind of bothers me about him—and I believe it bothers a lot of gals as well—is his front teeth. He just came into money—he's not the next J. Paul Getty, but he gave money to his daughter and son to help them out. Yet he hasn't thought of spending maybe a thousand dollars or so on his smile. This would help him look much nicer and raise his self-esteem, and of course the gals might be more interested in dating him. You may have been looking at that mug of yours in the mirror for so long that those holes between your teeth seem like beauty marks—wrong! Now, this may hurt, but wear a belt, and put that plumber's camera away. No one wants their picture taken by you.

I am a little vain, so I dye my hair a little. This is kind of like putting a new coat of paint on your old car.

My late wife once told me that a guy she had dated before she met me didn't dump out his ashtray in his pickup. She didn't smoke and was extrasensitive to cigarette odors. (She didn't like pickups either.) But I owe him a vote of thanks; I was the winner of that contest; we had a happy life together. I do have some disabilities, but they're not as bad as they could be; they're from the military, plus aging, and some parts are worn too. This can slow me down at times but by and large, they don't keep me from being selected by a reasonably large number of women, some as young as thirty-six to as old as eighty-two. I can't say I'm successful all the time or as much as I would like, but these women come from all education levels, professions, and career areas. A great many are ex-nurses, retired educators, bankers, real estate agents, cowgirls, Indian maidens, mermaids, and more.

You will find all colors, sizes, and religions on dating sites. Some of the gals have children at home or are living with adult children; others have children but are not living with them. It seems a large number have been married more than once, if not two or three times. They are active in assisting one or more of their children and are involved in raising their grandchildren. Some of them use this as an excuse why they don't have time to go out with you. Some have other activities, a family, maybe a job.

My new gal, as an example, plays golf sometimes, while I don't. She plays cards and spends time with and helps her family. Could it be that she's dating someone else and doesn't want to be with me? To tell the truth, I don't know; I have not been able to find out. But this comes into play as early as the first time you try to set a time and day for a meeting or date.

I call it the interview. This is when you come together for the first time after arranging a get-together at a location that is safe for both of you.

As a senior, you might not want to have more children. If this is you, then you need to make this clear. This is the first thing I try to establish. I try to make everything as clear as I can. I even document questions and answers. If you want to know something, you need to ask. Are you interested in getting married? If you are, but she isn't (or vice versa), you may be wasting your time and hers.

What does it mean when a gal says, "I am looking for a companion"? What does this mean to you? I am going to tell you my secret here. On occasion, I like to do more than hold hands, and if it's cold outside, I might be interested in more that another blanket.

I have met a few gals who—excuse me—seemed as if they had slept in that long, black, last-century–model dress. Sure, this is all superficial, but the truth is, just like in a job interview, the decision of whether you will get hired is made in just the first few minutes. The decisions in this complex thing called a date will be too. We all have something to learn, some of us more than others. You look at a woman, all of her, the way she dresses, talks, and more. And guys, the same thing is happening to us. You or she may not say much about these areas, but the meter is running.

I find dating somewhat different than when I went through this exercise about a quarter century ago. It seemed much easier back then, but we didn't use dating websites. We used newspapers classifieds to meet each other. We would call, talk a little, maybe write letters. Most of the time we'd meet at a coffeehouse, most often during the day, and we each would drive to meet at the place on which we had agreed and knew to be safe and, hopefully, not too noisy.

I can't say that I never was stood up back then, but the first meeting seemed much easier, with less information exchange and fewer games. We didn't always get a second and third meeting or date, but there seemed to be more meetings with each one than there are today. I have met in a woman's apartment as well as at a coffee house. There were fewer questions, less writing, less calling back and forth and changing days, times, and locations. It seems women want to know more about you today, and if you share a little more information, you are quizzed on this—it can seem like a quiz show: (1) If you had time off, what three things would you like to do? (2) How would your friends describe you? (3) Would you describe yourself as being romantic? (4) What are your hobbies?

I am not suggesting that this is good or bad. You usually will need to discuss, to some extent, your background and talk about some of your past relationships, your travels, children, career, and so forth. Still, I like to start from today's history and don't ask a lot of questions of my date. I tend to look down the road more and want to develop my own history with the gal I've selected. More than once, however, my date has been a little upset that I haven't quizzed her. I assume she thinks quizzing shows interest in her, and it does help me decide if this is the gal I want, regardless of whether she has an interesting background. You need to make you own assessments, though, and do what is important to you. At the same time, consider your date. You'll need to do this fast sometimes. That is just an example of what I do; you'll decide whether it's right or wrong for you.

I am testing various approaches—I'm doing this now with my new gal. A few days ago, I told her I had some things I wanted to talk to her about. When we met later that afternoon, I had two identical pages with written questions: one for her to fill in her answers and one that I had answered myself. I told her to look over her page and answer whichever questions she felt comfortable answering—she didn't have to answer if she didn't want to—and give it to me later. And I went over my answers with her. The questions covered trivial things, like *What is your shoe size?* or *How often to you change the oil in your car?* You'll need to come up with your own questions, and can be as personal as you care to be (for example, *Do you mind if I touch you?*).

When I first met one gal, Cindy, we went on a movie date. I kind of liked her. She had a nice figure; of course, we were both younger then. The theater was a little crowded, and people were having a hard time getting around each other, so I put my hands on Cindy's waist, intending to guide her so she wouldn't bump into anyone. She screamed at me, "Don't touch me!" First and last date. It had nothing to do with sex, and I suppose it was very personal. Still, I saw nothing wrong with trying to guide her through a crowd; we were both mature people. You must make these types of determinations yourself. It could it backfire, no question.

Because time can be limited, you may want to ask yourself if you really care for her. It's not so much whether or not she wants to marry you as how she feels about the concept of getting married again. If she's the right gal, come up with your own time period—months, weeks, or days.

Some guys and women are not into sex, but if you are, it would be interesting to know her feelings on this before you get too far down the road. What is too far—or not far enough? It could be never or it could be two weeks before you get married or engaged. If can be a hard question, but when is a good time to know? Personally, I want to know in a few months or less.

This what I call my philosophy. I try to explain my thinking, what I am looking for, what we both need to give up—like more time devoted to the potential of finding this person, friend, companion, and so forth. This may be a little task. I was with one gal, and she was stuck in her social life. She basically said this to me, and after that, I wasn't overly interested in her.

Some women say they are not interested in marriage; this is okay. They have their reasons for or against marriage. You must explore each—not only with yourself, but I would suggest with your lawyer. Now, I have a trust. This is my second one. I lost my wife to cancer after a four-year battle. You might be in a similar place—lonely, somewhat depressed; I have very few friends. You must judge for yourself, and take each situation into consideration. You may have children and other family members to consider, as well as your new relationship and your own feelings.

I have two kids who don't seem interested in talking, being close, or spending time with their father. I have offered to help to pay their way to visit me so I can have father/daughter time and father/son time. I've asked the youngest of the grandkids to come along too, as a family kind of thing to maximize the relationship. My point is that there may be issues with trust and—a big one—handling your wishes if you get ill and of course family valuables too.

Remember—some of these gals have been married two or three times, and I think we need to know that. I was married twice but would have stayed with either one. I'm not sure why the first marriage didn't work out, but as I've said, losing my second wife to cancer broke my heart more.

A number of women are very nice-looking, so I wonder why someone would want to give her up. (Someone knows; both parties know.) This could be a little scary because they might want to conceal the reason why a previous relationship failed. A couple of the women I talked to told me that their husbands cheated on them. I don't know if that was true or false, but we do know this happens. Some women are abused, but this could cut both ways. Some guys are married to their jobs. This can be a scary road to walk down. Some people are married to the bottle, the needle, or pharmaceuticals. I'm sure my first wife could come up with things about me, but as I've mentioned, I don't know what happened.

I have no idea how far I'll go with the woman I'm seeing now, but I do know I will tell her this: "From here on out, I don't want to know anything about any relationships beyond ours—yours and mine together. Everything before you met me is none of my business."

I believe this is fair. I am suggesting a clean slate. You, of course, can do whatever you want to do in this area. These are only my ideas, and in some cases, the things I have done and will do are trial and error.

Let's focus on getting started.

CHAPTER 2

THERE ARE SEVERAL types of dating sites from which to choose—Christian dating sites, "silver" dating sites, over-fifty sites. You may have heard of eharmony.com or Mate1.com, and you can discover a good many more. Also, there are sites that feature gals from Russia, Japan, India, China, and South America. I have used four different sites so far, but there are some you may not want to touch with a ten-foot pole. Once you sign up on one or two, you will open the gates to dozens, and you may not want to go there. I did this so you would know what to look out for and stay away from. As I said, if you look at one, the rest will follow. Once you click one, they can be a little hard to get away from. Also, you may fall prey to contacts from gals that you don't remember contacting—and that's because you didn't, but they are trying to hook in to you. If you fall for their scam, they will hook into you, so remember—an ounce of prevention.

I would also quickly assert that there are a good number of honest women seeking a viable relationship with a man. Having said this, once you find an honest woman, there is the compatibility sequence that we all must go through, and that compatibility routine requires some soul searching. Now, I am not suggesting that this is all on the women's side. I assume they are just as vulnerable as we are and face the same challenges, issues, and victimization. Therein lies the twisting road, as this takes time. Rarely does a rush job on anything hold up; it can't withstand the test of time.

Allow me to discuss this process that I used about twenty-three years ago. At the time it so successful that I married the gal and extremely happy with her; in fact, she helped save my backside. When I met her, she was divorced and had to nearly adult daughters, but I was never concerned about this.

I was divorced as well; as I mentioned, my first wife ended the marriage. I'll assume some of you guys have faced a similar dilemma. My first wife and I had two young-adult children; our daughter was married and living in another state, and our son was finishing college, completing his career in education. They had not been out of our home for long. At this time, we had recently purchased a new home in Southern California. I was having career problems but had gotten a position with a small manufacturing firm in a small community, about thirty miles away, as a sales and marketing director. I was trying to build business for the firm and a national sales representative team. I was the highest paid member of the company who wasn't a member of the family that own the firm. It really looked for me that things were turning around. I really like this job; I even used some of my son's girlfriends as sales models in my advertising program. This saved the company money and gave the girls some modeling and national sales magazine exposure too. I also had set up a national product-representative sales force for the company that had started to catch on.

But the downside was that the company was small, kind of new, and somewhat undercapitalized, and the economy was falling. As a result, I was laid off. I had no idea this would happen so quickly, but it did—something similar might have happened to you.

I asked my wife to go to counseling, and to her credit, we did go once. I wanted to do more; I didn't want to lose her. She was becoming a little distant.

My layoff hurt us financially, but she was safely employed. And she didn't want to go to any counseling. So, after about two years of my being upset and sleeping on the floor, she filed for divorce and moved across town. I did find some part-time work during this time—I taught at one or two junior colleges in the area—but one can't live on a part-time income. While I was teaching one evening, my wife took things from the house, where I still was living. Does this sound like something that has happen to you?

Once my wife moved out, however, I started to date as I could. At this time, most people tried to find someone through the newspaper classifieds, and I found a number of women around the area who agreed to meet me. There was a little discussion and, sometimes, a few phone calls, maybe a letter or two, but more than 75 percent of the time, whoever I called, I would end up meeting at least once. This meeting (which you might remember I called the "interview") might be the first time we saw each other, and sometimes I got turned down. Yes, we might have exchanged pictures, but photos don't always play in your favor—or the in other person's, for that matter. Normally the classified just had the person's name and a little about them. It might have read, for example, "Tall blond, forty-three years old, seeking tall gentlemen for dating. Call Jane" and then her phone number. Sometimes there also would be a photo.

This next information is hard to reveal, but I often was not sure if I could pay the dinner or if I'd have enough gas to get home. (Truly not a good time for me.) I don't believe anyone knew, but by the end of the day, it was my reality.

I was somewhat new to the Los Angeles area, and this was before the days of GPS. We instead used maps. If your eyes were bad or you were wearing glasses, you might find it kind of challenging to read the map. The LA area was (and is) quite large, so trying to find a location where we agreed to meet in Orange County, Riverside, San Bernardino, and so forth was part of the challenge.

I was seeing a number of women, although some just one time. I met a very nice gal (but a little young), who lived in the Pasadena area. First I had the issue of gas—she was about forty miles from me, one way. I have met women from fifty to over three hundred miles away. Eventually, I took the position that I would drive a little over fifty miles one way. This is a decision that you will have to make for yourself: how far are you willing to drive?

If there was something there—a spark or chemistry—I wanted to see my gal more than once a week. If I had to drive too far, however, by the time I got home, I'd forgotten why I wanted to see this lady. That's a little bit of a joke, but you get my point.

I eventually married the gal with whom I had the wonderful experience. She was, in my estimation, an outstanding woman—and, you might remember, she helped save my bacon. We were maybe sixty miles apart (she was in the Orange area, and I was in the Chino area).

For a little while, I did date a young lady from Los Angeles, a secretary in an insurance company. We used to go dancing, and sing to each other while we were dancing. One evening when I was with her, we were in the pool in the moonlight, just like in a romantic movie. I really liked her. She was nice-looking, and I felt I'd landed a great gal. Even though she lived sixty or more miles away, we grew very close very quickly. But then I got laid off, and when I called her to discuss our next date, she terminated our relationship. We had spent two or three nights together, and everything was positive, but my goose was cooked as soon as I lost my job. And I was back to square one.

My next relationship was with a gal in the movie business. After dating for a very short time, I moved in with her. I found out a week or so later that she was a little strange. We would go one walks and were getting along well, but she was very paranoid and a vegetarian too. She wanted to keep tabs on me all the time. Then I found out she was lying to me about her age and other things. One evening I moved out, and she started to attack me, screaming curses at me. I didn't say that all the gals I dated were sweet and wonderful, just that I was able to date more easily.

Very quickly I found someone new. At this time, days and days had gone by. I had been writing to dozens of so-called "qualified" women. I've been told that my profile is highly sought after and have scored, according to a ranking system, in the high eighties. I often wondered, though, if anyone ever looked at the scores. During my personal research, I never came up with real answers. The scoring seems to be so the sites can suggest someone for you—let's say that a woman with a BA in business who works in the advertising industry likes men with a little gray around the temples and who shine their shoes. Don't count on a good score on a dating site to attract potential partners.

Very shortly after I was dumped by the movie industry gal, I used the same classified-ad process and met a sex therapist (I'll call her Linda). She had her own nice car, which we used sometimes, but I had to drive to the LA area first to meet her. Linda taught me a few things I didn't know much about, and another time she took me to her office. But for some reason our relationship didn't last long. I liked her, not because of her experience, but because it was a matter of the heart.

I dated an attractive gal from the San Bernardino area, but only once. I had car trouble; the car thing was cutting into my dating. On top of everything else, I had another three jobs that didn't turn out well, and I crashed a 1965 collector Mustang, belonging to one of my employers. I was having a number of issues and had a few bad moments at the time.

But when I met my future wife, she allowed me to move in with her, and things started falling into place, and I never looked back. I considered it might be a scam; we genuinely cared for each other. It just felt so natural and real. I talked about marrying her. Although she was apprehensive at first, we were married three months later. She helped me get a part-time job in the medical industry, and then I got a good high school teaching position, and I started teaching college and graduate school part-time also. I also got a part-time teaching position in China and wrote and published some books—things were good. We got a new house together and eventually retired together and traveled a little. Even though losing her broke my heart, it was because of our positive relationship that I decided to try again. I believed maybe I could find other women as wonderful as my late wife, which brings me back to why I've written this book: to help you—and me too—in this search.

Facebook, emailing, and texting are all methods that may be subject to duplicity and deceit, but although other options, such as meeting face-to-face, are perhaps more viable, the latter takes much more time and is generally much less convenient.

Still, when you are across the table from someone, you can have eye contact, and this is something that is important. Be aware if she is not looking directly into your eyes, as eye contact depicts interest in you. If she won't look directly at you, I'd suggest that you be a little suspicious. Is she shuffles her feet, this is another indication of a lack of interest. And of course, if she looks at someone across the room instead of at you, you can pretty much assume that her interest is not with you. At your first meeting, you should have 100 percent of her attention. And of course, she should have yours too.

Most dating sites suggest that all women are different, but if they provide information with their profiles, you can hone in to select that "true" love. As I said, I have been on four dating sites, but I've failed to really evaluate someone or choose the right individual based on the scoring system. You are kind of on your own here.

The women generally are grouped together by the age range they prefer. Very little thought is given to geographic area. Gals have been suggested for me from New York, California, and the South Pacific, even though I indicated I have a dating radius of fewer than sixty. This goes for age also. I have suggested an age range of say sixty-five to seventy-seven but have seen ladies younger than my daughter, and she is fifty-six. Still, it's better than nothing. In my opinion, it's better to try more than one site so you can find one fits, and work with it.

You also can try real-life avenues, like clubs, at church, or through a friend.

For me, visiting dating sites often was a disappointing time, but I wasn't one to join the Bird Watching Society or a bridge club. I didn't hang at bars, and didn't have many friends. Someone suggested that I try to find someone at Walmart, or Albertsons, or at my gun club. I did meet a gal at Walmart, and we started talking. I asked her out and she said okay. Then we got around to the fact that she had a husband and that he was into guns but wasn't a very good shot I'm a member of the NRA, but I wasn't looking for some gal's husband to shoot me in the back or challenge me to a gun fight.

Not long ago, I went to my gun club in Fort Worth area, and I saw two nice gals in the cubical next to mine. I've been known to roll right up and introduce myself, so I did just that. I said hello and asked them if they had ever fired a weapon like the one I was holding, with a suppressor mounted on it. They said no, so I allowed the two gals to fire it. One of the gals in particular had caught my eye, so as she returned my gun, we talked about when they usually came shooting, which was on their lunch hour—they worked for an oil company. Although they both were too young for me, I said to the one I thought was very nice, "How about lunch sometime?" She agreed, but it never happened. I gave her my card—you should carry business cards and a pen as well—but I never heard from her. They were both young enough to be my granddaughters. I knew this up front, but it never hurts to try.

But I refused to give up. Over the next month, I tried the same thing a few times. I just needed to fine-tune my approach and targets. Sure enough, I met a couple of other women, and one of them stood out to me. She was seventy-two years old, about five foot three, and not bad looking. She said she came to the gun club about twice a month on Tuesdays. We talked, and I helped her with her stance and firing. I got to know her, and it looked promising, but she said she only wanted to be my friend. She liked my weapons, and I brought different models to the range every week or so. Still, I really wasn't looking for a *friend*. Then I found out she was married. She said she liked me and called me often to meet her at the club, but because she is married, she wouldn't go out. She said, "I can't go out on my husband. If I was married to you, you wouldn't like that, would you?" And the truth is no, I wouldn't. So good or bad, the sites might be the best after all. This sort of thing hasn't happened on a site yet.

But there seems to be a lesser degree of respect for the men. I have talked to a few women, and they have asked me what I think of this site or that site, and their views are a great deal like mine—they are not happy with the performance of the site, not the participants themselves.

It seems participants often don't tell the truth or give a definitive answer to many of the questions I ask, so often in seems like I'm flying blind. For example, it's important that you are informed if there is interest in you. So I might say, "If you are interested in talking to me, please email or meet me. Call, please, to let me know." I'd get no answer to that, not a word.

To be fair, some gals (an extremely low percentage) have told me, "I am sorry. I have met someone." And I thank them for their answers. If this is true, fine; if not, fine. I'll move on. On some occasions, I have said, "If it doesn't work out, let me know." Well, no one has taken me up on my offer later. How about this one: "I don't find us compatible"? I assumed all went well, based on my experience, but this is okay?

Overwhelmingly, I have gotten fewer positive responses than I did the first time around, back when we didn't have the organization, pictures, suggested questions, and so forth, but in general, we are the same people, just older and with more miles on us. But it seems that the participants somewhat hide behind their computer screens.

I have gotten more responses from women in all age ranges as pen pals or to talk as a friend on the phone or text. A large number of women from all over the country have asked me to meet them for coffee, lunch, or dinner, but here's the kicker. Less than 15 percent (I'm estimating) ever happen. It gets down to the wire, and they disappear. I met one gal I liked and tried to develop something with her. We had a second date for dinner, but she had an emergency and had to go out of town. I totally understood, and I kept in contact with her. Finally, she told me she was coming home and would let me know when she was back. I said, "When you have rested, we can go out." Now, this was over four weeks ago. She is still a Facebook friend but has never returned my call, text, or email. This seems to be a rule more often than an exception.

I met another gal—we met once. I didn't call her back right away, but I did a little later. She said she was going to visit out of state, so I contacted her a week or two later—and she told me she had given up men. I suggested that she reconsider, and she said, "Yes, but I have to go to Nebraska first. I'll will be back in about a month." I never heard from her again. As I said, these scenarios seem to be the rule.

I found a teacher on one site. She suggested that we meet and go out for lunch/dinner, but she said she had to go to Florida and would be gone for a month. I stayed in contact with her; I called her in Florida, and she said she would be back on a certain day. I suggested that after she was rested she should give me a call, and we would meet. It turned out to be a similar experience as I'd had previously—she couldn't meet because she was going to the New Mexico mountains because of her sinuses. She told me when she was due back. And she is back now, based on her schedule, but I have not heard a word from her.

I mention these situations because I never had such a lack of success in getting together for a date two decades ago. Something is different. There are more ways to see the person and put something together. I always ask the gal to select a place where she would feel comfortable, one where we can hear each other well. We meet in her town or city, and even though I may not know my way around, I now have GPS. I give her my cell number and the make and color of my vehicle. I am always early; most of the time I park in front of the restaurant. I dress nice, but many of these women don't know this because they don't show—this has happened too.

As I write this, I am working on a date in a few days, but I don't have her phone number or email. We are talking about meeting at a place near me, so it will be less inconvenient if she doesn't show. I have sent her several emails with the address of the location, the phone number, and directions on how to get there. I suggested she also could check the map on her phone. I have asked her to communicate by calling, texting, or sending email because the dating site is not working well, and I have no way of communicating with her if it fails again. I am thinking our date is this Thursday, but I've not had confirmation from her. So I am waiting for her to get back to me, and I'm not sure if she got my message. So we have these issues too.

I just went through this with other women; both had contacted me and asked if I would meet with them.

So I must ask you: if this guy is pretty much the same guy but a little older, what is happening here? Do I have to change my deodorant or my aftershave? I still bathe every day and twice on Sunday. I even brush my tongue—as you may know, it can generate a lot of bacteria. So, if I am the same guy, what has changed, as far as my ability to get a date? Sure, I have more gray hair, but I am still funny, still tall, and I now have $23.32 in the bank too.

I am going to continue to work on this question until I find a solution and can give you some clues (and the clues are for me too). I want to solve this dilemma. By golly, someone needs to help us here.

Here is an experience that I hated: I'll call her Ann. She had long blonde hair and was seventy-two years old and five foot six. I really like my gals a little taller, but for what it's worth, the dating site said,

"You are a great fit." This is if you can believe the site, and from my limited experience, you can't. Her profile indicates she has a master's degree, and if her photo is real, she is a knock-out. She is in real estate and loves business deals. She enjoys cooking for others, golf, swimming, and more. She enjoys American football and basketball—not important for me, but maybe you—and she also enjoys *Law and Order* (I do too). fiction, *The Tonight Show*. She's looking for romance and someone who cares. What can I say but sign me up?

Now here is the killer: she told me, "If you only were closer." She lives in Nashville and insisted that was just too far for me—it's several hundred miles.

This is this point you must remember: You are not alone. We all have our moments of duress. There were times when I was content to just sit and do nothing, not even listen to the radio or pursue a hobby or even read a book. I just sat, and it felt like I weighed a thousand pounds. This is a form of depression, and these events come and go in varying degrees in our lives. The better off we are—or think we are—the less likely we are to experience stress, but as human beings, we are all subject confrontations within ourselves.

CHAPTER 3

THERE ARE A rash of scams on the various dating sites.

I have been on at least four dating sites over the last two years. I am a senior, over sixty-five, a widower, and basically a young-looking, tall gentleman, not looking to hurt anyone. I hope to find a partner to share the balance of my life in truth, love, and happiness.

What have I discovered in the time I have been trying to find a new companion, friend, and maybe a new mate? At this point, young and middle-aged women have played with the strings of my heart to obtain whatever they can get from me.

Over this short period, six scams have been pulled on me. I am offered sweet talk and praise about my writing, a commitment to visit so we can maybe expand our relationship, and a suggestion of possibly a close physical experience, and more.

Normally, here's what transpires in my search for that special person: I try to put together a profile that depicts my philosophy and that projects what I am looking for overall. I describe my point of view and what I look like and enjoy. I display my humor and even suggest that I have two examples of what the new gal should look like.

The first example is this: five foot seven with long, dark-brown hair, brown eyes, and a little larger build but not bad. We use to dance a lot. She didn't smoke, drink, or swear. She was very outgoing and was the mother of my two children. She also was a teacher and worked with children. We camped, using a travel trailer.

The second example is this: five foot six, blonde, and with lighter skin. She was in nursing and was caring and very independent. She didn't smoke. She drank a little wine and a few margaritas, and she might have used a slightly off-color word. She didn't like to swim. We did travel but more by public transportation. She camped before I knew her. She had two daughters and was married before I met her.

Yes, my two wives are my basic examples. Why? It's very simple. I was with my first wife for over twenty-eight years and my second wife for twenty-three years. My first wife put up with a lot of my career changes and my going to school for several years. And we did move across country too many times because of me. However, we both agreed as some moves benefited me in my career. My children also played a large part in this relationship; they both helped put us in that situation. My first wife and I believed that the different environment would help us and benefit our kids. But it seemed that the moves didn't help the kids all that much; in fact, they developed some issues. In a lot of ways, it helped my career, but maybe one or two moves were too hasty on our part—we didn't see it right away; neither of us did. And I had a lot less patience then.

So, with my model in hand, I've tried to find a gal with that simple spark, looks, attitude, and patience. She doesn't have to have the same look, just pleasing to me. I believe that we all do this. The old saying is, "Beauty is in the eye of the beholder," and I say this is true. I am the first one to suggest that I am looking for a look.

I don't consciously think about this or compare in my mind how people look. There is a chemistry that happens, however, with the physical look that I see, but they don't all look the same.

Now, I find the gal who passes this test—again, this is not a conscious test. I examine the photo (hopefully. she has one there) and check the profile for various points—looks, age, maybe hair color, height. Hopefully she has more than one picture. Some do, many have none, and some may have pictures of flowers or their pet. What's worse (and does not do her any favors) is an out-of-focus picture, one that is dark or upside-down, or one that is too small to see what she looks like. Don't fall into the same crack. What I do, most of the time, is be nice but suggest that she send a new photo or two; often, she will. It is your choice, but you can stay away from those if you want; remember it is your call.

I am looking for a companion, but I have two dogs at home already. I am not interested in her dog, flowers, cats, or horses. I may make a comment that I had horses and used to ride. I don't mind sharing. It's important to tell the truth. It's easier and better, since you don't have to remember the lies you've told. I have no idea why they do this, but they do. Not all, well I can think of a few however.

Also, often in their statistics, they might suggest that they are about average in shape. They may have been at one time, but often the picture is dated. For example, one gal had a picture of her young daughter, and she was thirty years older and not close to what one might expect. Her picture was there, but from a much earlier time in her life. What is kind of sad is that some of these women were very attractive at one time, but for some reason, Mother Nature has not been to kind to them. Well, I am not as "hot" as I use to be either, but I don't believe presenting something that is not true; it is only going to eat your lunch later. And it's much harder to explain later than now.

Let's talk about the scamming. Here is how it goes—and remember it could change, but this has happened to me six times. The words may sound a little different, but they take you down this path in almost the same way. First, there is the getting-to-know-you stage.

In this stage she will want you to believe she's interested in you. She'll want to get to know your background. If it's a scam, she may send you a photo of a nice-looking woman, but more than likely it isn't her. It could be a guy scamming you, using a picture of his girlfriend or sister or a picture he found on the internet. The woman in the photo is more than likely younger looking than the age she's listed on her profile. I got photos from two very nice-looking gals, both of whom looked younger than they'd said, and they were appealing to me. You may buy into this, thinking that she really likes you. You may even believe that you are a hot "chick magnet"—most of the time, you are not—and you may not realize that this is a scam.

I've received a number of photos and a believable story from one woman. I didn't realize that "her" photos were stock pictures off the internet. A few days later, she said she wanted to communicate via Facebook Messenger. Usually I communicate by sending email; I had not used Messenger as a communication device. I was new to it and because I was trying to learn how to use it, there was more on my mind than thinking about a scam. In the process of working out how to use Messenger, I saw a nearly full page of her on Facebook—the same pictures that she had emailed me. As far as I was concerned, the scam had gone down. But now that I look back on it, what was it? Good question. At this time, I didn't know that this was any kind of scam. I was trying to meet this gal. I wanted to get to know her and have a new date, some romance, a girlfriend, a companion, and more. I was looking for a wife, not for a mystery or to be scammed.

In a phone conversation with her, I asked her to come up from Austin to meet me. I asked her, "Can you drive up?" She said no. As a gentleman, I didn't want her to drive up alone or take a bus or train by herself. But truthfully, I didn't want to drive down to Austin either. So I said to her, "Come up on the bus, and I will pay for a round-trip ticket. I'll also pay for your motel room, or you can stay in my guest room. And we can have a nice few days of getting to know one another. And if you stay in the guest room, we will have more money to use."

Now, I am not J. Paul Getty here; if I can save some money, that's super. But I would have put her up in a motel if my guest room didn't fit her needs and wants. In my mind, I was thinking of developing a relationship with this gal; I wasn't thinking of a sexual encounter. Yes, we were over twenty-one, but I hadn't done this before. I have had one or two gals at my place, and we got very friendly, so I wasn't beyond that, but this was not my first intention when I suggested she could stay in my guest room.

She agreed to come and said it would cost about eighty dollars, one way. I didn't know if that was right, but I agree on a hundred dollars one way and said I would send her two hundred dollars for a round-trip ticket. Then she said, "No, go to Walmart and get a cash card, and send me the PIN.

I said, "No, this is our first test."

She got mad and said, "You don't trust me. This discussion is about money, and I don't have the money."

I got weak for a moment—dumb, but I am only human—and I didn't really know we were on another page. I took a picture, and showed her four hundred-dollar bills. I said, "I have this in my pocket."

She hung up the phone on me. So I believed this was over. I'd lost my girl; she was gone, but at least I still had my money.

She was back the next day; she called about nine thirty in the morning and said, "Do you love me?"

I said, "No, I really don't know you yet. I have not seen you, held you, smelled you, and so on."

In fact, I had asked her earlier about another gal in one of the photos she'd sent. It had seemed to me, over the last few days, that I had been talking to two different women. One sounded American, and this gal sounded kind of European and was harder to understand. This started me thinking. Now, on this morning when she called, I was still sleeping. I am a little deaf from the navy, and my hearing aids were out. So I got up and went to my office phone because it also has a speaker and a reader. I put my aids in.

She then told me to go to Facebook and said, "I want to tell you a secret. My husband who passed away was rich. I want you to marry me. We can live together, happily ever after. But I need you send me the bus fare."

She told me she needed a lawyer, and I said, "I know a good lawyer in Denton, but you must get here. And I will help you like a friend. You can stay in my guestroom; it is nothing about sex."

At this time, I thought about getting the cops involved, because I was starting to think I was getting in over my head here, and I needed some advice. I called the police department, which was just down the street from my home, and asked if this situation was of any interest to them. They dispatched an officer to my home, and we reviewed the case. He gave me his email and name, and I developed an information package for them.

I later talked to the gal who had referred the "scam gal" to me—I'll call her Pat. I didn't actually know Pat because this was all on the net and through the dating site. It wasn't the site itself that was the problem, but I'd met Pat on the site. She had said that she was so impressed with my profile that she referred me to this second gal (I'll call her Mary), who was interested, lonely, and had lost her husband. She was from Denmark, and Pat said she needed to find someone to get serious with so she could stay in this country. Mary indicated that she didn't want to get married; this was not really her interest.

About a week after Pat introduced us, Mary called me, and we kind of hit it off. She told me that was staying in Austin, but I didn't know if she was by herself or with someone or when or if she needed to go back to Denmark. We started to communicate, by phone, Messenger, and email. We got very friendly, and I felt very positive about her. More and more, I really wanted to meet her. I was being sucked in, but I didn't realize it at the time. She sounded quite genuine, and I was falling for her a little. Sometimes we guys do this.

You must realize that I am an old gentleman, though young-looking. I am a former educator and entrepreneur. But more important to the scammer, I was a good target. Why? Because I had lost my wife two years earlier, as well as two other family members more recently, and I was extremely lonely.

Does this sound familiar to you? You might be in a similar situation. Please don't judge me until you walk in my moccasins. One thing I have going for me is that I have some experience with this type of situation and hope I now have a little more knowledge about it.

I want to encourage you to think about this dating thing with your brain, not your heart or other parts of your body. I've said this already, but it's so important that it's worth saying to yourself every time you look in the mirror. Maybe I should have said it to myself over fifty years ago when I met my first wife. But we were married for thirty years. I have these parts too.

By the way, since I was not socially connected to Mary, I decided to also work on Pat. I was not looking for a quick jump in the sack but a relationship. But no one told me this kind of scam was going on. I asked Pat if she thought Mary was on the level, and Pat said yes. Remember I was trying to date her too. I'd had so many ups and downs with different gals that I was trying to give myself some better numbers.

Yes, it's a numbers game; that's the bottom line. I will tell you my opinion all of the dating sites, although this may not be fair. I now have been on five different dating sites. The information I share is based on my experience. To tell the truth, I may decide to go on other sites until I reach my goal. Along the way, I might change my opinion of the sites.

Let's look at a few facts:

Let's say you've connected with a woman who is 150 miles away, and you have been communicating by phone, text, and email. This was my situation with Mary.

I had her information on my cell phone with her name and phone number. She'd also sent photos to my phone, but when she called, I hadn't seen these yet. She did send her photos in email, which I saw on my computer, and I did like what I saw. As I've mentioned, I found her on Facebook, and she helped me start to use Messenger to communicate with her.

Remember that one of the photos I saw showed two women—one blonde, one with dark-brown hair. I told Mary on the phone that I liked her hair but then asked if she was blonde or brunette. I didn't get a clear answer; it was like she wasn't sure. On the day she called me back—after the day she hung up on me—she didn't sound the same. She didn't speak as clearly, and she sounded older than she had on the previous day. I mentioned something I'd said earlier—about her being a "ten"—and she didn't seem to understand what I was talking about. It seemed not to register with her.

She again asked for money, saying she was angry with me but still would like to see me.

I said, "It isn't about the money." As you may see, at this point I didn't believe her. I was noticing inconsistencies, and I didn't trust her.

Bottom line: I wanted an explanation of the women in the photo. I didn't know the answer or why she had hung up on me. Should I believe her now? I didn't know.

She said she was in love with me and wanted me to pay her bus fare, and take me to a lawyer. She suggested sex and said she wanted to marry me and live happily ever after—if I would just help her get this money. She said she'd pay me back.

As I've mentioned, I met with a police officer, and I gave him about twelve pages of online conversation and emails I'd had with her. I did have all the photos, but if this was a scam, the photos could be changed. Still, I thought I could find her on the dating site; she should still be there.

I have been exposed to nearly four hundred women on five dating sites. They've been from all over the United States and a few other countries, but most have been from the Dallas/Fort Worth area, Oklahoma, California, the Midwest, and the South. I've talked about dating to over two hundred women and have met maybe five or six; I'm in the process of meeting more. They have an age range from over forty to over eighty.

Remember that you set the age range, but the sites aren't good at monitoring age range or don't seem to care a much. I've also mentioned that the sites score their members, but these scores don't mean much to most participants.

When I dated before, I talked to fewer women and met more. I dated for various lengths of time throughout the Los Angeles area. Some I dated only once and some for weeks. I lived with two of them for a time, and one I married. You can assume that I have some experience here. Some were a little older, and some were a little younger, and some I found very attractive. In my opinion, the various sites could do more with what women and men look like. This is a delicate area, and you may not like what I'm about to suggest, but this may save time: get the real date-seeker and keep her interested. And here is how. I believe that, as the saying goes, "Beauty is in the eye of the beholder." Then let's have the various sites set up photos of sample men and women—say, groups of five; these are stock samples—and maybe other related statistics, and the member can score these samples, by group or each individual, and the site will match the models to the score generated by the member, who then will be presented with individuals who best come close to the member's choice pick.

I'd estimate that more that 40 percent of the gals with whom I'm presented do not interest me because of looks alone—and I am not that picky. More than half have an undesirable location, and maybe 20 percent have an ethnicity that is undesirable to me. So we are wasting everyone's time.

Another Scam

Some months back, I developed (and continue to work on) my profile for the dating sites. My strategy is to present myself as honestly as I can and to cover those things that are important to me and that I believe will attract the kind of gal I'd like to meet, date, and maybe develop some kind of relationship.

At one point I believed I'd found this gal, but I was the target. We talked on the phone and emailed. We got friendly, and she told me I sounded nice and that I was the kind of guy she would like to meet. We talked above our backgrounds, histories, and where we were now. We asked the usual questions—where did you grow up? What kind of work do you do? Where did you go to school? Do you have a large family? What do you like to do? If you do this, as she gets to know you, you will get to know you her.

Again, as best you can on a computer, share pictures. Now, here is an important point: I got nice pictures of a gal—I'll call her Linda. She looked very nice, although a little young for her age. She said she was sixty-eight, but looked younger in her bathing suit and in shorts.

Linda said she was self-employed. I was confused because I assumed she lived in the area. This is something you need to focus on because you may be told that "Linda" is on an assignment out of the of country right now, and that's one of the reasons that you can't meet her.

Then she'll really start to work on you. "I dreamed about you last night," she'll say. "Your emails are great, honey, sweetheart. I'm out of town now, but I really want to see you. And as you know, I'm an independent contractor and to keep my business going, I need a certain machine. It only costs $1,500. Can you send me the money?"

Now the ball is in your court. You must decide if you're willing to spend the $1,500, which you may never see again. Will it break your heart if you find out she has been playing with your head and heart?

"Honey, this is very important to me," she might say. "I really need your help, and I then can come over for a few days to be with you."

This is how I handled it: I said no and goodbye.

Here is why you want to make it quick and fast—and absolute. She will start to play with your heartstrings. The longer you talk to her the more she will come up with the reasons to make you feel like a greedy bastard if you don't send her the money.

"You really don't love or care for me!" Let me give you this little piece to think about: she could be a guy! The "photo" on the dating site could be his partner, and they have other saps like you who they also are scamming.

Let's assume for a moment that they have three of you on the line each week or maybe more. If all three fall for this scam, that's $1,500 times three or $4,500 a week or $18,000 a month—or maybe more. Nice piece of change.

I want you to try this: say no and say goodbye. That was easy, smart, and saved you a few bucks too.

Yet Another Scam

Sue was a nice gal who looked very good to these sore eyes, and she was nice to talk to. We started off in the same way—friendly—and we get friendlier and eventually talked about getting together for a visit. At one point, she said to me, "When I get done with my business here, I am going to fly over to see you."

I was so gullible that I believed she had a pilot's license; this was based on the fact that I had several years' experience in aviation myself; when I got out of the navy, I took flying lessons.

You might be sucked in by her playing with your mind—you may think of those nice pictures she sent you (or *he* sent you, of his sister), and again she tells you how it is great to talk to you, how handsome you look, how good your writing is. Of course, you want to hear this stuff too.

And we men believe this until we find out otherwise. I know I did. I think there must be a school someplace where they learn this sort of chat because when you compare the stories from different scammers, they sound very much the same in the flow and timing until they get to the close.

In this case, she said she wanted to come over, but she had creditors after her and needed a few thousand. When I asked her where she was, she said Cincinnati. I thought she was in Texas. And no, she didn't have a pilot's license; she was going to fly on a commercial airline.

When she asked for thousands, I didn't question it. I said yes and sent it to her. And then it was over—with that cash out of pocket.

I can assure you if you try to question her story that she will come after you with, "You need to trust me"; "You don't really care"; "You don't really love me"; or "You need to have faith in me—and us."

Yes, I stayed on the line a little longer than I should have with this one, and she started trying to negotiate for a smaller sum, but how do you know it isn't going to escalate? She may ask you to get a cash card from Walmart and give her the PIN. This may sound crazy, but it could happen to you.

We were talking again about her visiting me, and I then discovered that she was in Austin—I saw her Facebook page. It had four photos of her, but she didn't look the same as those she sent to cell phone. This was confusing, and I hadn't had the chance to ask why this was so.

Now let me share this with you: she called me twice to say she missed me and that she would call me later this evening. What was this all about? I had asked her to visit me in Fort Worth, which is over 150 miles from where she is, and she said no. A few days later, she indicated a visit would be OK. She said she didn't drive but would take the bus—if I sent her a hundred dollars for bus fare. I agreed.

Remember that I still trusted her. Still, when she asked me to send the money, I said, "No, I'll give it to you when you get here."

She said, "Don't you have the money?"

I said I had four hundred in my pocket, and I repeated that I'd give it to her when you got here. Then she asked me to send her fifty dollars. Again, I said no.

She got angry, saying, "You don't have the money! How much do you have? I have two houses!" And I thought, *Two houses but you don't have a hundred dollars?*

Then she asked, "What is your net worth?" She asked related questions, and she was mad.

As you can see, there was a lot at stake here. If this happens to you, remember that it's not just bus fare. It could be your personal finances.

My Final Example

All the scams seem to have a commonality of walking you down the primrose lane, trying to get your trust, interest, and love. Then, once this is accomplished, the scammer will say she wants to be with you or offer any kind of relationship you want.

I don't know what the top end of this could be, but we can assume that some scammers get thousands of dollars from unsuspecting men. As I said, use your head when you are dating, not just your heart. If the relationship seems too good to be true, or if it sounds untrue, or it seems to develop really quick, it more than likely is a scam.

Remember Mary, the woman from Denmark? Here's more information to consider if you connect with someone like her: First, what mature women would call you up on Sunday morning at nine o'clock to talk? In my case, I had not met her yet; we'd only talked. She also said, "Do you love me?" How would you answer this, or would you answer at all? I did for two reasons: (1) I always told the truth, and (2) I was collecting information on her. As well as sharing this, I want to learn how to be smarter.

As I've mentioned, my answer to her question of whether I loved her was, "No, not yet. I don't really know you and haven't seen you, met you, touched you, held you, or smelled you. Now this isn't about sex.".

Early on, she mentioned not wanting to get married, but she suggested that she might have to go back to her home country if she didn't. But these were separate conversations at different times.

Since I understood that she was talking about living together and maybe getting married, I focused on the fact that I had been married twice and had two children, and no one seemed to complain. I was trying to compare my other experiences and use good sense. And I came to the conclusion that I needed some help. That's why I called the police. I was a little embarrassed, as you might be, but remember—if you are right, this could save you a lot of money and embarrassment down the road. Sure, you deserve to meet a nice gal; we should believe and understand that. It's suggested in the Bible that man should have woman, so basically, we are on the right track.

CHAPTER 4

C URRENTLY, I'M WORKING on developing relationships with two different women. They are both in the Dallas/Fort Worth area. One is sixty-nine; I'm not sure of the other one's age. I'm in the interview stage with both, and I am talking to more women each day. Some are not bad, some are nice, and some not so much. Some live close to me, so we can easily meet. Others live miles away some—135 to 350 miles away. Even when they live that far away, I do try to answer them. I try to answer others who may be too young or too old—a nice answer, with a little humor. For example, if she is a little young, I will tell her that I have a daughter older than she is, and then say, "I'm not sure that you would like to date your dad."

Each one of these seniors has a little problem. Try not to insult the women or make them mad, but you need to address each issue. If you find someone who is pleasing to you but too far away, you might say, "Thank you for your response, and I would be delighted to meet you, but we are probably too far apart to meet."

I also tell them, "I am in the Dallas/Fort Worth area," so they have an idea of where I live in relationship to them. I'm not suggesting that you do this, but I have not had a issue with giving a general area where I live, especially when we start talking about meeting. A number of the women will be willing to drive halfway to meet you the first time. I prefer picking them up at their place, but this usually is not acceptable on the first few dates. Back in the "good old days," we almost always picked up our dates at their home and returned them there. Now women are more cautious, particularly with someone they've met online.

I was lucky enough to date a gal recently; the date was a long time in the making. I offered to pick her up at home and added, "I'm Jack the Ripper." She had a positive response to that, and then I said, "But Jack the Ripper would tell you that too." Is this a sign of the times? I always suggested this in the past. Am I the only one who wanted to pick her up and take her home?

Another Scam

As I was writing this book, I was almost victim to another scam. I didn't know it at the time, of course, but several weeks ago, I got a phone message from a woman I'll call Nancy, asking "Why didn't you return my call?" At first I couldn't put the name her to the call, and I didn't remember calling a Nancy. Still, I decided to pursue her a little. I had nothing going on for a few days. I do get a few calls from women, and this one who called sounded very nice.

When I called, I was joking with her, and I believe that upset her because she hung up. I called back and apologized on her message machine because she didn't answer. Anyway, I tried to get reasonable information from her—what she looked like, her age, and so forth, and I asked for a photo. In the process of chatting back and forth, Nancy asked if I needed help with sending her a photo of me. She talked me through it, and after a few minutes, I sent her a picture of me. We discussed our ages, and after I saw Nancy's photo—and realizing that she looks very young; a nice-looking blonde from Africa—I asked her why she would be interested in a seventy-eight-year-old, even one who looks, on a good day, like he's sixty-five.

Surprisingly, she had a good answer: "Age is just a number." She said something about two people falling in love and caring for one another, so age didn't matter. Then she talked about coming over here ("I want to see you, baby"). Not many women call me baby, but I tried to keep my mind clear—and I started to get the picture.

"How are you going to get here?" I asked.

"I'll have to renew my passport. That will cost five hundred dollars."

We were getting into the basic back-out-nicely stuff. I said, "I need to be able to see my gal two to three times a week to get to know her, to develop our relationship. How are we going to do this?"

(As a side note, early on, I asked her point-blank, "Is this a scam?" Nancy asked me, "What is a scam?")

She went on about needing love, and I said I understood.

You need love too; a lot of us need love. I do too—but I'm not looking to lose my house in the process.

She said, "We need to help each other."

I said, "If you were here, you could have a place to stay, food, and so forth." And then I said, "How are you going to get here? Swim?"

She said "It would cost five hundred dollars or more."

And I told her goodbye.

Then she called back and said that Nancy wasn't her real name and that she was going to use another name on her passport, but before she could explain, I was gone.

I could have made copies of this information and passed it along to the police, and I have given information like this to the FBI. You can contact the FBI online and file a complaint; there is a little paperwork involved, so you'll need to decide if you want to do this, but I will offer this advice: *terminate* your involvement with the woman as soon as it looks like or feels like a scam.

If anyone asks you for any money for a bus ticket, taxi, motel, or anything, the answer is *no*. Hang up. Also be cautious about giving out family information, such as if she asks, "What's your mother's name?" You can find information on the internet about almost everyone. I can find all my twelve of my wives, for example, and the name of all seventeen of my children, their ages, and where they live. Of course I made a joke of it, but it's true—I recently went online and found information on my half-sister (who is deceased), my first wife, my daughter, my son and where he works, and I found it within at no cost.

Save any correspondence you may have with the potential scammer. Back in the good old days, I never once had this kind of issue. But we are not living in the good old days, are we? You recall that I told you that I got off on the wrong foot with another gal who called me, and I apologized to her on her answering machine. She never called me back, but she did ask me if I was scamming her—she had been on the dating site only a few days. I tried to prove to her I wasn't a scammer, but she didn't think I was funny; maybe she was too thin-skinned.

If you do give some gal money—as I said, please *don't*, but if you do—do your best to ID the process. Write down the numbers of the bills, the debit card name and number, the PIN for a cash card, and anything else that would help the authorities to apprehend the scammer.

What You Can Count On

Only you can choose how many dating sites you want to try and which ones to keep active. It's a matter of economics. I have no idea which is best for me, as new ones are available all the time. It takes a little time to learn how to manage each site, as they are all a little different (though similar) in the way they work.

Once you decide which one to use, I'd suggest that you choose a simple password. (In fact, the new approach to passwords is "keep it simple.") I am slowly moving in this direction, as it was too much of an issue for me to remember all the passwords I had for different sites. One or two good ones is all you need. If I were to do it over, I would use the same password for all the sites that I am on—something that is easy to use and easy remember but hard for others to discover.

I also would suggest that you take good-quality, current photos in several flattering poses. Dress up somewhat formal for a few photos, and then take informal photos when you are, for example, traveling, off-roading, playing a sport, hiking, boating, dancing, and so forth. This is especially a good idea if you are going to say that these are some of your interests. All of the photos need to be the best you can get.

I would say one of the biggest mistakes people make is that they offer photos from several years ago, or the shot is from the waist up. I like to see her face, hair, and a full-length picture too, so I can see how she dresses. This reminds me of a gal I met who looked like a bag lady. Most men want to see the women they are trying to contact. There seem to be a large number of gals with no photo at all.

We know that beauty is in the eye of the beholder, but she will want to see you too. I am not going to tell you to bang your drum, but if you are going to a gunfight, don't take a knife. Is it safe to assume you have an idea of the "look" you're hoping for in a gal? I do! And they have an idea of what they want too. If nothing else, why join a dating site and look like the Witches of Eastwick? It's your money, but would you go fishing without a fishing lure?

When I was in sales, marketing, and education, I had maybe five suits. I was called a "clothing horse." I suggest that you buy something that you look good in, and go work out too.

Work on your attitude. My opinion is that until you meet and really talk to someone across a table, you won't know if she is a "match." That's because the "experts" don't have a clue; in most cases, neither do we. And before you go "shopping" for a companion, you must find room in your heart. Take time to drive it around … or it will rust and die or run away.

In developing your profile, you should include some of the things that women look for in a man. In my opinion, it's better to tell the truth or say nothing at all. I was an athlete in high school and junior college. I followed my son's football scholarship career, and I coached a girls' and boys' school, but I am not into pro sports today; this is not important to me. Women don't need to bait my hook; I don't fish. To me a gal who is flexible is more attractive to me. She may not like to go fishing or to the gun range, but she is willing to go to a home show or, as my dear late wife would do, see a political event. I really didn't like to go, but I would not say anything. I would just go and enjoy her over dinner.

Someone recently told me that women in an Arizona retirement community are looking for younger men to accompany them on several sea cruises, as older guys get sick and have more physical issues. My position is that I am not interested in anyone who want to use me. Maybe I should go after younger women because they look younger and can be more fun. In fact, I was invited to visit this retirement community because there are hundreds of these so-called rich women. But I was not interested in this view.

We may face many women on the dating sites who subscribe to this same philosophy, so you must be careful. I am looking for women who want me to share love and then share what I have. This may not be true for you, but that's how I feel about it.

As I have suggested, work on a good profile about yourself. Talk about your views, physical assets, and things you like to do, such as flying, travel, boating, reading, or going to museums. Your physical assets are your height, weight, and color of hair and eyes. Mention whether or not you smoke, as many women are looking for nonsmokers who do not do drugs. I have run into some women who have unwavering political opinions, and if you do not agree with the political party they support, then they are not interested in you. This isn't always an issue; my second wife was more conservative than I was, but that didn't affect our relationship. It's up to you whether having similar political views is important.

CHAPTER 5

L ET'S REVIEW MY dating system. This is not cast in concrete, but I think it works—not as good as I would like, although I don't know if the fault is mine or the system's or the women's. I am still polishing it up, but I lean toward blaming it on the gal's issues. As I have indicated, when I was dating decades ago, it was much easier. I would select the picture of a gal but had very little to go on—just a few personal statistics and a phone number.

Each week I might get three or four women a day who would like to meet me—and that's not counting the gals who send their profile in with more of a shotgun approach. On each site, you will get a "heart" or something similar sent to you to indicate that someone wants to hear from you—but this may not be true. I'm not totally sure of the site's screening because some women will say, "I don't think that we are compatible." I'm not sure how they can make this judgment without talking face-to-face, but that's basically what they say. Or they don't respond at all. Or they say they've found someone, we're too far apart, or "You are too old." These, at least, are the good ones because you kind of know where they stand.

As I've mentioned, I have tried to suggest that I don't want to hear from or date gals who live much farther away than sixty miles or who are any age other than from sixty-seven to seventy-eight. I have tried to date or meet women who are farther away, but it has not worked to well for me. I leave the rest open. I may tailor a short introduction for the gal when I contact her, but otherwise I have a canned profile and presentation. I try to continue working on it, making it sound better and checking the spelling. I need to get it to say what I really want and mean. It still needs a little work and also needs to be the right length.

There are several deviations that you might try; for example, you could tailor it toward a certain type of woman, like the vegetarian, or the athletic type, or a special religious group. Some women say they are the outdoors-type, or they really enjoy traveling and talk a lot about where they have been and would like to go.

Every so often, women will ask me if I would like to meet them for coffee, lunch, or dinner. This is where it gets kind of interesting and frustrating at the same time. We are communicating on the same message site, but sometimes the site administrator will send you a message that someone is interested in you, and this may be the same person mentioned in a different message. I find the sites can be less than accurate in some cases. It seems as if the site has a number of women they are having trouble matching up with anyone and so it continues to market them, push them onto you over and over again. Some are nice-looking, so there expectations may be too high or outrageous.

In my opinion, something is up here. The site may have twenty-five or more of these gals, and often they will never get back to me. Maybe they will call you, and you may have the magic touch. For example, of the "twenty-three women that you might find interesting" (according to the site administrator), there may be one who agrees to meet with you. The first thing I like to do is communicate through email and then on the phone. The main reason is that some of the messages you send on the site don't reach the gal in a timely fashion, so you have greater control if use email or even Facebook Messenger. You can send pictures or videos too.

I also have been working on getting Skype. I like the concept because it's live video. You can use it at no cost, but obviously you both have to have it. Sometimes it seems the other person doesn't get the message that I'm calling until it's too late. One gal told me she had to cancel our video date because she didn't get the message. But if you can talk on the phone or live Messenger from Facebook, live is better. You will have more control and feel better too.

I had a first-time date arranged, and overnight, she disappeared. Her photo is still up on the dating site, but I've had no communication from her at all. I had talked to her. and she'd suggested that she was interested in meeting me. We arranged a date, but the next time we talked, she said that she was putting away some Christmas stuff in the garage, and a box fell and hit her head, and she was feeling dizzy. Our first-time date was coming up in a few days, but that was the last time I heard from her. I tried to contact her, but she was gone.

As I've mentioned, I'm working on two different women. I've had as many as three at a time, just trying to meet for the first time. Some disappear out of town, or the dates keep changing, or important information gets mixed up, delayed, lost, or dumped.

I have this one I kind of like, but I have not seen or been with her yet. The days and times keep changing, or there's family business, card games, church activities, work, and so forth. We were to meet here soon, but I have lost her. No answer from her site, even though she generated our getting together. I tried to get her to contact me through my site or on the phone. This is the second time this has happened.

So you may be a casualty of the dating site.

I am really looking for one gal. The last time I did this, it was one at a time. We seemed to be able to pick one day, one location and time, and we both showed up there. Remember that mentioned buying flowers? I assume not many guys do this, but women appreciate this gesture. If you buy her flowers, I think it sets you apart, and it might make the difference in whether there's a second date or not.

I am open nearly every day and evening for a get-together. I have appointments or errands but I'm very flexible on the day and time to meet someone. I have a hobby on which I spend a few hours of week, but if I have a meeting or date during this period, I make it clear that the date comes first.

Are you willing to meet a gal who lived up to two hundred (or more) more miles away? I've talked to several at this distance. One was over 150 miles away, and I almost went for it, but in talking to her, she said could not move. I can, but would I? Could you, if this came up? How much driving back and forth as you build the relationship are you willing to do? What about finances? How often do you want to see her, go to her, and so forth? It's better to come up with this answer now. You can always change your mind, but I know I want to see my gal maybe two or three times a week. If she lives far away, it could be fifty dollars in gas for one round trip. Then I'd want to take her to dinner. That could be $145. (This was the price of a dinner recently.) And of course I'd get her flowers—that's about twelve dollars. So unless you are independently wealthy, you may have a little cash flow issue. That's why I've set my range. It's food for thought. (But maybe you can get her to pack a lunch.)

Most of these gals seem loving, romantic (so I am told), and understanding. They like to cuddle and hold hands, most like to cook, and some like to travel. They may have a cat or dog and like movies, western music, and eating out. They like to laugh, are family-oriented, and like to spend an evening at home reading a book. Some like fishing and boating and professional sports. I like to go to the gun club twice a week, but I am flexible. I also like wild hog hunting. I really don't like fishing. I do like dinner out, dancing, and live theater. I'm not much on casinos. You should tailor this to yourself or what you are looking for.

One thing that most women seem to have in common is they all want to travel. You will need to come up with a list because they will ask you, as well as asking about your background. They like to hear little adventure stories, like how you and General Custer were at the Little Big Horn together or at San Juan Hill with President Teddy Roosevelt. If you have a good story, like from rags to riches, this will be welcome too!

Here is one example that I used many years ago. My mother would often take me down to Missouri, near where she grew up, and we would stay with one of her friends on the farm. In those days, I got a little practice in milking cows by hand, going after the cows, and even using the hay baler. We lived near Des Moines, Iowa, and one day, my dad brought home a piglet for me to raise ... and I did.

Women will tell you some of the places they have gone, where they grew up, or something about their families. You may want to reciprocate by telling about your background, and if you have some common background, this goes over well. They will talk about sports to gain your interest, as most men like sports.

Remember that flowers can improve your chances for a second date. I do believe this helped me—I think my being able to get two wives speaks for itself.

CHAPTER 6

WHAT DO YOU want to use for a rating system? I try to use the information that I have. As an example, if the gal likes to ride horses and has a ranch or farm, and you had a horse at one time, I'd suggest that you use to own horse story. Don't make things up, but if you have a connection, talk about it.

Here's a little story I tell about my daughter, who was a professional model in the Bay Area of California, with regard to horses. I had to discuss with her what would make her feel better about an upcoming move, and she said, "Buy me a horse." Not only was this the truth, but it added a little family flair to my story. We did ride in Utah. And sometime later, my second wife and I use to ranch alpacas in California.

There will be a little background in her story—where she is from, what she did with her family. You will understand a little about why she is on a dating site—the loss of her husband or family, something about why she is now divorced, and so on. She also may talk about how long she has been a widow and that she now has decided to get on with her life. Or maybe she is not happy being alone. When a gal presents herself in a way that she is not, however, and you do this too, this puts you on the same level with her.

In my case, I shared some of the story of my loss. I wanted to give the honest reason why I chose a dating site. My heart was in the right place, and I was looking to move forward; I had a hole that I believed I needed to fill.

As of this writing, I am emailing with a gal I like the best. I haven't met her, but there seems to be a lot of interest on her side, and we have been messaging back and forth. For more than two weeks, she was out of town, then back, then busy. Finally, we had zeroed in on a date, time, and place. I tried to suggest nicely that we should communicate by email or phone—because as I've mentioned, the dating site messaging seems unreliable—but she seems to be intentionally not getting back to me in a timely manner. When this occurs, it's easy to miss the meeting or date.

About two months ago, I found this young lady on one of the sites. She looked young but not too young. From her profile picture, which was not a close-up picture, I suspected that she was a little heavy. Some guys like gals who are a little heavy. Others prefer someone who is tall, short, skinny, or athletic. I played football, track, and basketball in high school and college. Does this make me athletic? If so, I need to change my profile information.

We met anyway. I decided to be as fair and as honest as I could be. Honestly, she didn't fit my model—remember I gave you that information? I believe we need to have some idea of what we are looking for, and there are a number of areas that are important; appearance is one of those for me. Also, I prefer a gal who is taller than five feet—I'm six foot three.

I haven't danced in a long time, but I like it, and many women do. This is also something you need to put in your profit, along with the kind of music you like. I like old rock 'n' roll but not the Beatles or heavy metal. I also like folk music and big band. I might sing a few lyrics from an old big-band song or name of one of my favorite entertainers, like Bill Haley, Little Richard, or Frank Sinatra.

One gal I met for one date was OK, but I was looking for someone else, although I didn't know who. A few weeks later, I said to myself, "Call Jane, and ask her out again." I needed a date. Jane was the one who told me, as you might remember, that she had "given up on men," and I told her to give it some thought before she made that decision.

Jane was out of state—at least she told me she was—and now she said she had to go to Nebraska and would be back on a certain day. You also might remember that when that date came, I suggested going out once she was rested, but I never heard from her again. I'm still not sure what this means. As I've said, I bathe every day, shave every day, and always dress nicely for a date.

Another time I met a gal, "Sandy," and we arranged several dates that she had to cancel. She had a daughter at home who needed help with babysitting, and situations came up that she couldn't resolve. Sandy and I really hit it off—or so I thought—but when I asked her about going out on the second date, she said, "I must think about it. You kind of remind me of my old boyfriend." She said she liked me, but we never went on that second date.

I might talk to five or six gals on Monday, and a few ask to meet me, but by Friday, I have none and must start over. I'm telling you this because we need to work together to come up strategies so this doesn't happen.

I was dancing in Los Angeles, making out in Riverside, and dining out with a young gal in Ontario. She had two kids, and we use to make out in her driveway. I took her a few places, and I liked her, but she was a smoker and also had a problem getting away from her kids.

I hope we can all do a better job, as I have suggested. I am trying new approaches, ideas, and strategies. Some of you may like to deviate from the standard procedures if that works better for you. Or I can help you go down a path that is better for you.

The next situation I'm going to share with you is something men often encounter. A woman I'll call Denise was nice-looking and seventy-seven years old. She lived near me, which was a real plus. I was surprised when I first asked here where she was from and realized we were in close proximity to each other—maybe forty miles apart. I told her I was looking for a nice, great gal to build a solid relationship with, and this was true. I suggested that if she didn't have the time or was too busy with other things that I wasn't interested in talking to her and that I was not interested in her money. I mentioned this because a gal recently had asked me to help pay her bills so she could fly over to visit me. I was serious, but she was seriously after my money. I even shared the fact that I had been scammed about five times.

I again said that I was interested in a good relationship. I wanted to have some fun, travel some, and go to museums, the fair, and state shows, and have romance too. (Most women's profiles indicate they want romance, togetherness, holding hands, and such.) I talked about how long I had been in the area. I mentioned losing my wife in the context of Denise and I both having lost someone very close to us.

Often these women will discuss how long they have been a widow, and then I respond with how long I've been a widower. They may often talk about being lonely. This is your chance to relate your experience in this area. Most of the time, they appreciate your showing your feminine side. It's up to you, but I believe this will help you get close to your women of interest.

It has been very challenging for me to find someone on the dating sites, to the point that I have asked myself, "What is going on here?" At first I got a lot of positive responses, but a few women would ask me if my messages were canned. Yes, they were. If you are writing something to five or six women a day, do you want to remember the same story and rewrite it for each one? I say no. So not I admitted up front that my message was canned, but I tried to improve it. I found that when you write something over and over, you often have typos. So I tried to write something original to each gal because they are a little different. For some women, I commented that I liked the color of their hair. I also like tall gals. I usually don't pursue a woman who is short. I tell the truth, because then I don't have to remember what I've said. The truth will set you free.

A good many women are out of my dating range, and I deal with this but thank them for sending me an interest notice. I also often apologize for not being able to meet them because of the distance—any farther than fifty miles away just doesn't gel. I still communicate with a couple of gals—one in Saint Louis and another in West Texas—who keep sending me messages. I answer them because being an ass is not going to win you a popularity contest. Three or four others want to correspond with me, and I send them something if they ask me or tell me something. "You get more flies with honey than you do with vinegar."

I have received accolades from the one of the sites, telling me that I have a very popular profile. I am not in competition with anyone, but I would say that a good percentage of women can relate to me, and they agree with a lot of what I say. They like the fact that I have indicated what I am looking for in a women. I continue to work on my dating site profile.

I recently met two nice women, using my own material that I have shared with you here. They were both similar, not surprisingly. One was seventy-two years old and a widow. I kind of liked her, and we seemed to get along well. I forgot to buy flowers for her—although I did find a flower shop after the date—but we had a very nice meal in an upscale restaurant (yes, a little pricey). We decided to get together again for a second date.

A few days later, I had a first meeting with the other woman. She was seventy-seven but looked a little younger. I got along well with her too. I got along with both of them, but I was drawn to the second gal. Still, I am having some issues. I liked her, and we seemed to have fun together, but that was only the first meeting. I let both gals select the restaurant, and we discussed what we like to eat. I am very flexible, so I said I would eat anything. One was a vegetarian and the other had shrimp. (I really don't care. I can assure you I miss very few meals.)

On each we went to places I had never gone before. Thank goodness for GPS. As a younger man, I lived in the Bay Area and in Southern California, but I did a lot or driving around both areas. Here in the Fort Worth/Dallas area, there is a lot of building going on, as well as a new freeway, and they keep changing the roads. Even a GPS may not know all the changes, u need to watch what is going on and what is there.

I had no idea where I was going, but I made it to both dates on time. I always try to leave early and park in front, but I must find the front first. Often I feel that the GPS is taking me the long way, but I can't make changes because I don't know where I am half of the time.

As of this writing, I have another date with the first gal, though it's unconfirmed. I want that date to be at a special location because she is special to me. We have talked about possibly more dates in the future.

Anyway, this is the plan. You also might find someone who quickly becomes special.

I did say I liked the vegetarian—let's call her Sally—and have been in communication with her. We have talked a few times back and forth, and then I lost her for a while—she said it was due to family business. I actually know very little about her, but I do know that she showed up early for our first meeting, and if she tells me she is going to call you at five o'clock but is late, she apologizes for it. As of this writing, we are planning two or three more different dates. Sally contacted me on the dating site, and I am trying to get her to use my email or call me on my land line. I've mentioned that if the dating site goes down, we could miss a message. If we use email, this breaks us away from the pack, and we have a little more control. You may come up with your own reasons for not using the dating site messaging.

The truth is, I am only interested in finding one woman. I hope I can find the right one. I'm not trying to manage a harem of gals, and I don't want to spend a lot of time on it. I just want one nice gal. If you think this is what you are interested in and want, then go for it.

Sally had another issue that came up and said she would get back to me. This could be very true; I have no idea. She is being honest and truthful, and I am not locked in to my vegetarian yet. At the same time, I don't want to lose the opportunity to meet Sally. She could be the right one. I have no idea. It's a matter of keeping the communication lines open, so I am going to do this. As a man of my word, I have not given it yet, so it is open season on trying to find the right relationship.

CHAPTER 7

RECENTLY I FOUND someone who I believed was a nice gal, and she lived only fifteen or twenty miles away. We both knew the area well, so I thought, *This is going to work.* We planned to meet at an Olive Garden. My plan, as always, was to get there early. I have handicapped licenses plate—I have a bad back from the military—so I could park near the entrance. I went in before the designated time and told the hostesses that I was waiting for my date and that I would be sitting by the door. Six o'clock—our designated time—rolled around, but no one was there. I checked to see if anyone had asked for me—I am very hard to miss in my clown suit. No, I wasn't wearing a clown suit, but I told the young lady what I would be wearing and that I'd park my fire engine–red Ford F-150 in front of the restaurant.

Later, when I talked to her, she said I wasn't there. I didn't see her, and I had described her to the hostesses. I have no idea what happened, but I was able to recover. It didn't work out, so my advice to you is to have a plan worked out for you and the gal you are going to meet. I thought I did!

I am going to share a good experience that I believe was on the right track. I believed I'd found a gal to be serious with, and this is what I wanted. Let's call her Val. She was seventy-seven, within my preferred age range. I like blondes, but Val had brown hair. I like tall gals, and Val was about five foot seven. I not into really overweight women—not saying anything good or bad about anyone, but this a fact. I try to stay open to all religions and most ethnic groups. I really don't care about someone's career, but my first wife was a teacher and the second was a top nurse, so there's is a place to start. I was surprised that lot of gals on the senior dating sites are still working. I'd like to find someone I can see and be with a lot. I am retired and have a lot of free time. I have a hobby or two, but I really like women. I'm not some kind of sex addict, but besides loving them and holding them, I like their touch and scent. You get my point here.

Some women are involved in a lot of stuff—church, family, friends, volunteer work, and so on. The gal I am trying reel in has some family responsibilities. On one hand, I have to give them a lot of credit, but I am looking out for me.

Anyway, at this point, I found out that Val was in real estate and seemed very independent. I personally like that. I really don't want to date a gal who is so dependent that she can't pump her own gas. My first wife was a plumber, and I could deal with that. She wanted to use her own name on stuff, had her name on accounts, handled all the insurance papers. She believed that she was good at it, and she was, and it was something I didn't have to do. She took care of the yard too.

Anyway, I dated Val, and it felt good. We went out a few times. I went over to her place, and here is one thing that helped me decide about her.

First, understand that I liked her, but she lived eighty-five miles from me. You may have to make this decision—"Do I stay with her when she lives so far away?" What is your next move? I didn't want to invest a lot of time in this relationship if it wasn't going anywhere. I enjoyed eating out with her, and we did one family activity—a family Easter egg hunt. Everyone was friendly, and I talked to her brother about wild hog hunting, since I enjoy this, and it was a way to get closer to her family.

When I took her to my gun club, she seemed to have a great time and was smiling and happy. I really believed we had a connection.

The next time I called her, I asked if she might be interested in getting closer to me. I said I really liked her but was interested in more. She said no; she liked me but wanted to continue to be my friend. She didn't say it was too early or she needed more time or wasn't interested in marriage—although at the time, I wasn't presenting that scenario, nor did I suggest getting engaged.

She didn't ask, "What are you talking about, interested in, or suggesting?" My thinking was that a friend is a person you might go with to the gun show or the mall, not one you neck with. Oh, I enjoyed kissing this gal; there was no issue with that.

So dating her was over, but I even called her back. I wanted at least what I'd had. I wasn't doing so well without her.

It seems that once you have the formula that works for you, more than ten ladies may be interested in you. For example, Karen thought she knew what she was looking for in someone. She was seventy years old, five foot seven, nonreligious, had a master's degree, and was involved in art work, gardening, walking, sewing, and cooking. She was a retired public school teacher with long blonde hair. She felt that she passionate and seemed to be very loving, but she had lost two husbands. One of the big issues for me was that she was out of the metropolitan area. I didn't really know her agenda; she said she was looking for someone, and that was great, but how long would this take to gel, and how much would it cost to put something together?

Do you think you can develop a relationship on the phone or by computer, and how often do you need to see her? As I've mentioned, I'd like to visit several times a week, as well as talk on the phone. She was in Arkansas, and I'm in Fort Worth. This is two to three hundred miles. You can talk on the phone and send love letters in email, and even video chat. This could work; I have no idea. She believed that the distance wasn't too far.

As I've said, I had no idea where this was going. I suggested that I had a new girlfriend who lived closer. She had a job, and her family lived near. She tried to help a somewhat disabled family member, and she played cards once a week with friends. She went to stage shows and movies with other lady friends. Can this gal have similar responsibilities? Sure, but more than likely not.

Another women who was about 250 miles away said she had business in her area—she had an economic relationship with her brother and could not move away. So besides back and forth travel, in the long term are you willing to move? I can, but do I want to? While you are dating, will you visit for a few days there and a few days at your place?

My new girlfriend came over to my place. We had a date to go to my gun club to shoot and later go to dinner and talk at my place. She drove about fifty miles one way, and in that one time, she believed it was kind of far away. What do you think? I thought so too. I would be driving back and forth, and this was only a hundred-mile round trip. For the other women, it would be five hundred miles for one date, even if I stayed over. My long-distance relationship lasted maybe a week, and I didn't even get a kiss. So now my range is sixty miles or less.

As of this writing, I'm talking to another gal. She's a teacher but works only a few days a week as an English professor. She is outgoing, and again, beauty is in the eye of the beholder. One of the things we must do is put up more current pictures, but I am going to say that fair to me might be outstanding to you. But to keep it simple, I might meet her and might not. She teaches college in the area and is involved in her homeowners association. I've been involved in that, and it can be a lot of work.

But what I like about this gal is that we are geographically close. She is looking for a kind, open, honest, and affection relationship. I am in a little dilemma because so am I. Maybe we all are. She has traveled a lot in the United States. and Europe and some in Asia. She is not into politics or arguing religion—my kind of gal, here; me too. She really likes dogs too.

Here is a point to consider: many of these women sound good, just like many of us guys, but which ones really mean what they say? Or do they say what they think we guys want to hear? I don't have an answer; you'll have to find out for yourself by testing the water.

Let's look at Helen—seventy-four years old, a good number for me (how about you?). She lived forty-seven miles away from me, so I don't know. Her body type was listed as "average"—not totally sure what this is. Truthfully, I must see the gal, and if she looks good to me, this is my real indicator. Nice legs, good posture, and I really like long blonde hair; soft, not all tight, and not dull-looking. Kids not at home—at my age, this shouldn't be an issue, but it might be for you. College graduate, nonsmoking—this is a deal-breaker for me. Smoking helped to kill my mother and father at an early age. A Christian—I really don't care, but again this is a decision you must make.

Helen has lived in Texas for about twelve years—me too. She also had some experience in Miami when she worked in the cruise industry. Is this comment true, or is she fishing? She likes dining out, does volunteer work, and likes camping and canoeing. I not much into camping, unless I have my twenty-six-foot camper. And canoeing—I don't swim well, so I will pass on this too! And cooking with friends? Maybe if she cooks, I will eat. Music, movies (this is very generic). I like a good western, science fiction, navy SEALs, mystery—this would be more clarifying. Anything on or near the water—this interesting and maybe great. My second wife really didn't like to get wet.

Her ideal date is dinner or lunch, so we can talk. This is nice, but if you ask me out, please pay the bill; this would make me happier. Question here: how much is real, and how much is wishful thinking or fishing? I have no idea, but you can find nearly the same information with every gal that sets up a profit.

Let's call this nice gal Sam. She responded to me with the following:

> Thank you for your interest. We are nearly 4 hrs apart. Too far. I did specify 50–100 miles no further, and they keep giving me fellows 4, 5, 6 hrs away. You seem very nice and I wish you luck.

I see this comment a great deal, and many, as far as I am concerned, qualified as a date, but I find out for myself that we have this distance thing.

If you are in a large metropolitan area, like San Francisco or LA, this would not be such an issue because of the number of women per square mile. I don't know this number, but when I was dating about twenty-five years ago, this wasn't an issue, and today, the population of these areas has increased, so I am going to assume it even might be better. I am sure the dating population in the Dallas/Fort Worth has improved too. You will just have to work out the advantages and disadvantages and work from there.

Look at Jan's response to me:

> Ranching seems to be important to you. I only have one
> pair of boots and they are 25 years old. Just broken in. I am
> not ready for a cowboy. Sorry. Thanks for the text though.

This was a clear case of one of us missing the boat. This is why it is extremely important that you clearly understand what this lady is looking for, and it's also extremely important that you are clear on what you are searching for and can express it in terms that the gal understands. I wasn't really going after Jan, but wanted to leave the door open because I am not totally sure that the person I am working with and I are really into each other. And Jan and I are on totally different pages with our searches. Finding the right group of gals is not an easy take.

Then there's Sandi—seventy-two, five foot two, short blonde hair, retired, Christian, has a master's degree. Not bad for starters. She's looking for a relationship, but what does this mean to her? You will have to find out for yourself. But let's see what we have here. She lives in Kingwood. I don't have the foggiest idea where that is located. You may have to search for yourself. She does seem very attractive, neat, classy, and loves to laugh, and lets her emotions hangout. She's caring and is very romantic. She enjoys, movies, traveling, music, dancing, and some sports. It is going to be up to you to find out what kind, which one, and where she would like to go! But this may be an issue. She responded to me in this way:

> You are a nice man. I have met someone very special. I
> will be off this site at the end of the month. Thank you for
> considering me as someone you might want to meet.

This could be a genuine story—or not. You may never get a chance to find out.

My new gal doesn't like meat; I do. She's not active in her religion; I am not either. I like cookies and Pepsi; she drinks water. This saves me money. And I like the way she kisses … We are both conservatives, and we both like to shoot at the gun range. And this is rarely mentioned. But I will bet you this is more real, and she likes cooking for friends.

Here's another example to deal with, another response I received:

> I guess I am confused as don't know what you mean around 50 [miles]. I would like to know more about you before we meet so we have a mutual understanding of what we want. If you are looking for someone younger I won't waste your time.

Barb is five foot seven, and as I've mentioned, I like tall women. I like to dance, and so does she. My parts are from a '39 Ford, and I look like a '65 Cadillac, but I still have a lot of old parts.

But Sam tried to sell what she has but didn't offer a photo. She is a Christian with a high school diploma. She enjoys playing computer games in her leisure time, which seems more like a sixteen-year-old. Gee whiz, she is seventy-two and lives in Bonham—I have no idea where that is located. She's knock-out, but I may lose interest fast. How about you? But she does like visiting family. The second plus is that she is seventy-two, but I don't have much to go on here.

She's looking for a relationship with companionship and loyalty. I think we all want this. She wants a guy with a good sense of humor. It seems about 85 percent or more want a guy who is funny. Several women have told me this. So are you funny? Roger Dangerfield was, but he isn't around, so you might have a chance here.

And Sam enjoys traveling, dining out, and cooking, and so do I, especially if someone else is picking up the tab. I would say that over 95 percent of the women like to travel or talk this story. And dining out— just last week I took a gal out, and I should have known better. When I saw the guys in penguin outfits, I knew it was going to be somewhat pricey—over $150, and no gravy for my smashed potatoes either. She is easygoing, caring, and loyal. What do you think? Does she blow you away? Not me. I need a picture too, and maybe not even then.

Here's a nice-looking blonde with long hair, but let's exam this candidate. Right out of the box, she is only twenty-five miles from me—this is great. She is five foot three, average build, attended college—does this mean she has a degree and a career? Maybe not. She doesn't smoke and is a Catholic. Does this mean that she only will date in her religious group? If she will talk to you, you might find out.

But before I got to talk with her, she asked, "Did you write a novel?"

I always try to tell the truth, so I said, "No, I wrote and published four books. One I use in my high school vocational, classroom, and three were published and still sell but are dated, but they were self-help for career. I used them in an adult education program and sold nationally to the general public.

She said, "Not interested. Goodbye. Please don't write again."

I didn't claim to be Hemingway. The books were sold throughout the USA, and I sold some in Saudi Arabia too. But she is sixty-six. I am sure she is a lovely woman too.

CHAPTER 8

TO CONTINUE, MARTIE sent me the following:

> Dear Gene,
> Thank you so much for your message. I know I am looking for someone. I am an eternal optimist. I have been widowed twice and loved both men passionately. I am in the country west of Hot Springs, Arkansas so not an immeasurable distance from Fort Worth. I love to garden, am an artist, seamstress and reader. Also, can put out a good meal. I am devoted to all my interests and super devoted to my pet babies. I have two dogs, one cat, and one tiny kitten that are all rescues. See if there's anything you like here and let me know.
>
> Martie

A seamstress is a one-person kind of job/hobby—not much there for a man and a woman. Reading, too, and artist—here again, is she up to dealing with a man/woman relationship? You may need to ask her where you would fit in to this relationship, if there is any.

Here's another:

Gene: Thank you for your letter. I did not know you are Navy, good for you! I stopped reading after you said, "we are too far apart". Good luck in your search for that special someone!

Yep—I agree. it is 125 miles—so too far for me for sure. Thanks though.

This one was from Karen:

Take one day at a time! Much like you, I love my little dog, but it's not the same. See where life takes you … you seem to be a very caring man. Nothing wrong with tearing up when you were lucky enough to have a great marriage.

Still shed tears when I think of my loss. nothing wrong with it! Makes you a caring and special person!

Let's look at Bee:

Hi Gene,

I am very new to all this social media. I am a recent widow.

My husband of 34 years passed away about 7 months ago. I am realtor, I live in San Angelo, Tx. I feel bad for you for some of your past experiences. I don't like drama, only looking for someone to share some time with, doing things that both enjoy.

I am also a one-man woman also!

I have a couple of question for you. Bee looks like a intelligent gal, passionate and honest. But I would like to know what she meant when she wrote, "Share some time with." When I was in high school, this is what we did, but I want a serious relationship—from traveling, to sharing problems, to making love, and everything in between. But this isn't what I am looking for. You have to ask what is a deal-maker and deal-breaker for you?

Here's a long message I received from Kay:

I told Deb you live in Tx. She was in hopes this was too far to come. She knew both men I married. She doesn't think I'm a good judge of men. I told her you weren't interest in marriage or visiting. Likes you better already

My daughter Debra Jean 60 David R (Dave) 56 Rick 54. He is paramedic. He works 3 county units. He calls like this morning at 3:50m small roads in Ky. Worries me. He drove wrecker for us till 2006. Papa's open heart. Rick took over the Wreckers. I closed the auto sales. I could do everything but go buy. We had opened the transport. Contract with post office 10 yrs. Picked up US MAIL in Big Spring carried to Midland. I drove the mail some to Ackley north on US 87. twice a day. I should have paid me. Papa was engaged for 3 years. Paid her bills. I have gone over it so many times. I had Mother and the 3 kids. and I really did love him. I don't know why. We carried VA patience from hospital to hospital. or nursing home. We carried blood and or drugs. He liked anything with wheels.

We went to WV ever year. Had to have a new vehicle to go in. He told his aunt he had to be something for me. Without me he could have gone to WV and his cousin and him could have sit under tree & drank. Never knew he felt the pressure. The women didn't expect anything.

After that, I received the following:

8:07 p.m.
I find that sad. I don't see me that way.

8:08 p.m.
I'll think about you at lunch. Otherwise I'd have to eat alone. Deb and a friend are going to lunch and she's going to bring me lunch I will share.

9:56 a.m.
We had a chicken fry, grave, mashed potatoes salad, Tea. In case you forgot,

Peggy

He had 3 stripes. 3 days before payday. He had 5 guys for cards. Fix something. It was baby food or think of something. made a really large biscuit no tomato sauce. Pork-n-beans onion tomato little hamburger couple cans of something. They were nice Best pizza they had. They may not have eaten in days. Peggy

5:09 p.m.
Got it!

5:55 p.m.
Aug 16, 2018

good afternoon ran across your photo I had computer problem and was checking to see what was missing

Karen, 5-0" HS, Catholic Mistakes ... OMG ... did publishing work, the last nine working years was putting a 14-page newsletter together every month! I should not make typo errors! I will call but must be out and about this afternoon. I must pick my granddaughter up from school and I need to go grocery shopping today. It has already been a busy morning. I appreciate your giving me your phone number. At least Texas is not in the path of Florence! That is one thing that I don't have to worry about since moving to Texas!

Would like to meet someone with a sense of humor! Is passionate about music too.

Carol,
I will call this evening if ok, I'm working today.

I noted that she lives in Fort Worth, is five foot four, Christian, master's degree.

She seems to be honest, cuddling, and sees herself as a good communicator.

Here is a little from Randi, a realtor, seventy years old, and nice-looking, based on her photo, which a good many women don't provide the first time. I am not sure why, but I have asked, and you can ask too. She's five foot ten, Christian, a high school graduate, Caucasian. She is in good health and is very optimistic and looks toward the future. And finally, she is passionate about music, family, and love. Sound like a good place to start.

One of the biggest recurring issues with many of these women is the following, as stated by Randi:

> I was thinking the same thing. It's over 230 miles. Probably too much distance. You sound interesting, I hope the best for you. Good luck with your search. Be careful.

I must assume that a good many of these gals are out of range for me. You will have to make this decision for yourself. This can very frustrating and disappointing. I see nothing here that can help, depending on how interested you are in finding a significant other. Join more than one site, although that can be pricey, or do a little more research on the best site to meet your needs. I have not done this.

Let's look at a message from Beth:

> Yes, I still have my business and intend to keep it as it's lucrative for me. I appreciate your honesty. I'm *not* moving from my historical home in Seguin or the Cabin Hideaway in the New Mexico mountains during the summer heat and humidity because of my asthma. I'm looking for a companion that is a good conversationalist and can travel who enjoys similar activities. Thanks for your honesty!
>
> July 23, 2018
> You "viewed" me? Why?

And here is a piece from Ann:

> You definitely have a sense of humor. That's an asset. You sound active in your life and ready to enjoy all that life has to offer. yes, I'm sure we could spend considerable time

sharing stories. We both have a lifetime of stories to share. I never square danced but did a little dancing in my time and I still enjoy that. Thank you for your service in the navy. An admirable thing to give. Good luck to you in finding what you're looking for in your date with Mary. I wish you well. Have fun! And don't forget your oxygen mask. Lol

Here is Foxy:

What are you talking about? I never sent you anything other than a smile.

To be honest, with Foxy, not to offend her or any of the other ladies to whom I might send my "canned response," I sent her another response. I was just fishing, and I didn't mean that in any negative manner. I try to find women I might find attractive to send my response. Sometimes it works; sometimes not, but my goal is to attempt to establish a common dialogue and in some cases, if possible, set up a meeting. I don't think you can get to know someone from reading someone's message. They may mean well, but it just may not make it clear who they are or what they are looking for, even if they try their best to express it.

CHAPTER 9

I WAS NOT CONVINCED I should publish the following information. It isn't because I don't enjoy sex or have an objection at all. It wasn't to promote this book as sex tool either. Looking back, I am generally pleased with the relationships I had with both of my wives—the first, the mother of my two adult children; the second, with whom I had a good and healthy relationship. I never went out on her, seeking another women's love or a relationship. My only regret is that she was taken from me to soon.

I was not with another lover for over six years during our fight with her cancer and after I lost her. When my first wife left me, however, I did indeed have a few encounters. I could have used a few pointers, so I'm assuming maybe you could use a few too.

The first thing you need to do is respect an older woman's privacy. When a few guys get together and have a few beers, often the talk of conquests starts to evolve. This may not be a very personal thing to you, but it is to many older women. So keep your mouth shut. Most women want to be comfortable in knowing that the you are not going to tell the whole world.

Women want to know that you respect them enough not to be running off at the mouth about them. I am not very creative with pickup lines; I never can remember the whole story. In fact, I sometimes tell a group of men and women that I always have to come up with new stories because I forget the punch line all the time. Just start a casual conversation about something you may think of and build on it. In my limited experience, I have found that older women are attracted to creativity.

A lot of guys often forget this point: women are human beings too. And like everyone else, women vary from one to the other. I was invited to a very attractive gal's home in the Los Angeles area, and we were in her front room, talking. She simply got up and said, "Come with me." I knew she wasn't talking to anyone else; I was the only one there, and I did.

A lot of women do not like to talk to guys who keep changing the subject from one thing and back to sex. One key thing is to listen to what they are saying.

What do older women (or all women) like to see in a man? They have said the following:

1. He makes me believe that I am the most beautiful woman he has ever met.
2. He makes me laugh. (This is very, very important.)
3. He is intellectual.
4. He is a witty and sharp guy.
5. He makes me feel like a women.
6. He is masculine.
7. He is willing to listen and not impatiently offer oversimplified answers and solutions.
8. He is willing to communicate if he is upset; he also offers opportunities to make it right and does not use the silent treatment.
9. He is willing to stand up for me.
10. He is emotionally stable.
11. He doesn't gets hung up with games that females may try to play and is willing to call them out but with respect.
12. He knows how to take control and make decisions.
13. He is willing to say what he means and mean what he says.
14. He understands me.

15. He trusts me and is secure in himself and in who I am.
16. He lets me casually molest him.
17. He wants to give me the world (even if he can only give me his heart).
18. He is playful and creative sexually and has no boundaries in the bedroom.
19. He has a nice smile and hair I can pull.
20. He doesn't whine about my choice in friends and realizes he doesn't have to spend time with them; he can choose his own.
21. He treats his mother with respect.
22. He makes me feel completely new but more like myself than I've ever been.
23. He is a good kisser with good personal hygiene.
24. He cooks for me and tries his best.
25. He asks for my opinion.
26. He is romantic and poetic.
27. He is faithful.
28. He doesn't disrespect me to other women and keeps his flirtations innocent; he is charming and will not be owned.
29. He provides sex on demand, unless I don't feel like it, in which case we snuggle and read together.

Now let's look at a moment on the other side of the bed. What do older men want in a woman? We older guys have our own definition of what a hot and sexy woman looks like. In many cases, many older guys are looking for younger women, but it is also true that many older women are looking for younger guys. One reason is that older guys are still interested in engaging in sex. And they have an idea locked in their minds of what still turns them on.

Often these men will move from one relationship to another. If one doesn't work, just jump in to another one. Dating coaches will advise women not to get involved with men until they have a year of being single after a divorce—sort of a cooling-off period.

As men get older, what they want often changes, and they have less time to play games or be superficial. Here are some of the things that women can do to make themselves more interesting and attractive to older men:

- They should try to make themselves look more attractive. I am not saying they should try to be twenty years old again. That's not what we are looking for. Guys need to find something that is calling out to them or is alluring about the woman.

- They should take care of themselves. Of course, they might not be the same size or weight as they were when they were younger, but neither are we men. But if they eat well and get regular exercise, it shows.

- They should try to have a nice smile: Women who make themselves approachable by smiling and appearing friendly and enthusiastic are much more attractive to older men.

- They should try to make the man feel like a man. Some expect older men to be women in men's clothing, but men our age often have a preoccupation with their own interests and masculinity.

- They should not play games. Honesty and respect is important, with no drama and no games. As an example, I dated a young gal, and the next thing I knew, she had to go out of town. I contacted her when she returned, and she said she had given up on men. I hoped she would reconsider, but I never heard from her again.

- They should not be too serious. It's best to try to relax and seek companionship based on shared values and common interests. I met a gal who was into competition shotgun training and development; I'm interested in tactical weapons training competition. I thought that was interesting and a really good match. I offered to help her, but after talking to her and working together to help here, I never heard from her again.

- They should know what they want from a man. What really makes him special? They should have some idea of what is non-negotiable—the deal-breakers, the things that absolutely make them not want to date a man. But how many of these things are truly non-negotiable, and which things are not that important? I have found that a number of women are not willing to give up that Thursday girls' night, the golf game, and so forth.

- They should try not to set too many conditions on a new relationship and be open-minded about what is their "ideal" man or perfect relationship. For my part, this has never crossed my mind.

Some Tips for Older Women

It's sad but true that older gentleman have more issues with sex than women of about any age. So their dealing with this issue may be more valuable. It is not necessary to give up on something that is enjoyable for both people in a variety of ways, but at the same time, it can be disappointing and heartbreaking. This can be so disappointing that both parties could walk away sad and unhappy.

What can be done? Most men may not be open to talking about their erection problems. Erectile dysfunction (ED) can vary with age, but it doesn't come automatically with age—the dysfunction is not a normal part of aging. It is clearly an unrelated issue associated with other health issues.

Women can help their mates by talking about ED and learning something about it together. If they really care about their partners, this can rejuvenate the relationship and their sex life again because it can die off over the years. Together, learn about various causes and alternatives, from pills to various foods to injections.

Extra pounds can have a toll on your sex life, so women and men should work out together. I used to swim as my second wife ran around the track at our retirement community. This can help.

Women should remember they aren't just helping their mates; besides the sex angle, they also are helping to improve their own heath.

Cholesterol levels and diabetes both can lead to erection issues. And a waist size over forty inches is more likely to increase the problem with erections. Quit smoking; this will help in reducing erectile dysfunction.

Women and men can get involved in hand massage, and fellatio can be one of the cornerstones to great sex. This can provide both men and women pleasure.

The key is to enjoy a good relationship. It has to be a partnership between a man and his woman, working together to please one another. Part of this pleasure comes from good communication, both ways. It is going to take both physical and emotional adjustments, but once you both master the techniques, you'll be on the trail to mutually fulfilling lovemaking and happiness for the rest of your lives. One of the biggest keys is working and loving together.

CHAPTER 10

HERE ARE MORE messages I've received from women in whom I've been interested:

> Aug 13, 2018
> The Japanese sounds wonderful but let's save it for dinner. I am not hard to please food-wise. I have a GPS, so I'll come to your end of town. Crab shack would be great, of course it might be noisy. Oh, well. I cannot venture to your end of town until Thursday, 30th. If you send me address and name of place, I'll be there!

This never happened, and two weeks later, I received the following:

> So sorry, stuff happening here so I need to postpone Thurs! Will get back with you later in the week!

This also never happened. Not only that, but three weeks later, I still hadn't heard from her. I wondered if she had been run over by a car. If she did, I would feel bad for criticizing, but a simple phone call wouldn't have been too much—even a note to say, "Gee whiz, I found someone else that is better looking and has more money than you." Say something.

> Just saw your message and I completely understand, I usually disregard a person who is more than 50 miles from San Antonio, TX. Once again, I wish you luck in finding someone you can get interested in that lives near enough to you. I hope I find the same.

> Hi! I saw your profile on line. We seem to be looking for most of the same things. I have been widowed since 2009 after 50 years, not sure how this works as it is the first time I have thought having someone else in my life. If you are interested in more communication, please let me know. If I don't hear from you, I wish you all the luck in the world finding what you are looking for.

> I live near Texarkana, in AR. At this point I basically go to church and Bible study, help with a food pantry and, today, a clothing ministry. I *like* doing many of the same things you do, but not alone. I am flexible and really like to travel. … I grew up traveling. We were missionaries in Scotland for 3 years. That was fun, but hard in ways. My book tells it all, my life, that is. Sara "Ann"

> Gene, I think you are right that the distance would be a challenge. My sister lives in Grapevine. If I should get down that way, I will let you know and maybe we could me for coffee, lunch or dinner.

Get statistics on the gal's age, hair color, height, education and such. And here's a few more gals too …

Judy is five foot five, curvy, widowed, a retired school teacher, independent, and a Lutheran looking for friendship and companionship. She just want a traveling companion. What does that really mean? But she wants no drama in her life. And you guys who smoke—this is a deal-breaker. I have to say good for her, but this may "fry your fish."

> Hi Gene

I have my grandkids this weekend so not a good time for me—let's shoot for next week!! Sounds like you have a lot going on so no problem with a bit of a wait on your end. :-) Hope not anyway.

Thank you for replying. Yes, we are a long way apart. I truly hope you find the lady that will make your life a singing joy. You deserve it. If you ever need someone to talk with, great.

Jeanne

Sounds good. I just tried to text you but would not send. Anyway, I just wanted to know what LL means in your last text??

If you are wondering, "LL" means land line. At this point, I have found no reason to criticize this gal. She has done everything I asked of her. I am still waiting for the other shoe to drop. I have told a couple of my friends that this experience has made me paranoid. As I've said, the first time I was trying to find a new girlfriend, it was one call, one meeting.

8:21 p.m.
Gene, I am in a relationship Good luck!
I used to go to firing range in Abilene but no longer have a gun.

Hello Gene,
Thank you very much for the interest and for taking the time to contact me. Immediately after I joined the site I started corresponding with someone and we decided to find out what is going to happen. Honesty and faithfulness is one of my best qualities, so I apologize for not being available at the moment. I wish you all the best, hope is what will keep us living the present but visualizing the future.

Sorry, I don't see us as a match. Thanks.

You have written quite an extensive letter of what you are looking for here. This is my very first experience with this type of adventure. I've never looked before, nor put myself out there to meet someone. I just decided it would be fun to meet someone to have fun with. Do things and go places with. I don't think the computer can do much other that match people up. Personal meetings will tell the truth. Pictures, mine anyway are current, and my hairdresser knows how to take care of that grey hair. Your philosophy is interesting. A topic for good conversation.

You are way too far away. I live in NW Arkansas!

8:42 p.m.
Sent you a smile!
Gene,
Do you really think so?

Martha is five foot three, has a master's degree and is a retired teacher and administrator. She is respectful of all people, concerned for the poor and the oppressed. Loyal to her friends. She is looking for someone who is honest, willing to do things with her, someone interesting and "not always wanting to grope me."

Hey thanks for the post. I'm in Cuero about seven hours away. I try to stay within a hundred miles to be able to visit more. Good luck in your search.

I am happy for you, Gene. You are lucky! I have only made one contact via this dating/internet way. He was nice enough, grabbed my hand while he walked me to my car, our first meeting, and then he was all over me. I was embarrassed and took myself off the website. But still would enjoy real companionship, love if it comes. But even though I have been alone for many years, I still have a need to care again about someone! I truly appreciate you writing, most wouldn't. Says a lot about the man you are, I wish you love!

Karen

Hello Gene, did you get my message yesterday? Why do you call yourself crazy legs? Beth

I am divorced for 18 years after being married for 16 yr and lived together for 3 … I am an independent woman after retiring from AT&T with 45 yrs with them … I was a manager for them for 30 yrs … with what I think is a "Practical experience master's degree" … I was used as a problem solver … then as a manager for their emergency power equipment and DC equip for the central office equip … at one time had 2 crews totaling 24 employees and 90 offices covering most of North Central Texas …

August 7, 2018
I live between Burleson and Mansfield … Been retired 7 years … have dogs, horses … still love both … love to read, play computer games to keep my brain active and sharp … I love to dance, swim, table shuffleboard … U don't like the truth or my opinion … don't ask … Trump girl … not much upsets me anymore … I used to think I was 42' tall and invincible … now 5'3" and size 18 … not svelte but clean up very nice I've been told and I know which fork to use when out and about … my phone is dying … need to charge … will call U later if ok … There are two things in the world i hate!!! thieves and liars … I will not tolerate … and I do not like users … I always look at my glass as being almost full … I always try, not always successful, to see and be positive!!!! I believe totally in my Lord and Savior, Jesus Christ … I am not a Bible thumper, nor a fanatic and not in church every time the doors open … if u like what u've read so far … please let me know and I will call later … if ok with u … I do think I'm easy to get along with … and I really try to be … I've been successful in my job … being a top manager, and a reserve world champion running barrels … sorry this is all over the place … but trying to give u an insight as to who I am … because like u said … it takes two to tango (which i do not know how to do … LOL) oh … one more thing … I've never been able to vacation or travel anywhere without horses … I think I would love

to travel, experience life and fun things … but I need an entertainment director … to be my partner in crime … I'm ready for a relationship … and my profile picture was taken late winter, early spring 2018 …

August 7, 2018
So UR reply is U R not interested and do not want to go further … I'm not hurt at all if u r not interested … It is just one of life's bumps in the road ..if u don't … u don't … I wish u well.
Penelope

Penelope seemed very serious about getting together. Right or wrong, I really didn't find her overwhelmingly attractive, certainly not enough to jump into my pickup anytime soon to race down to Louisiana. If she'd lived closer—twenty-five to fifty miles—I might have felt differently about it. She said she loved horses, dogs, and water and was very flexible. But she was not a young gal. She stated that she was curvy and five foot three. I like my women a little taller, and for me, she was a little heavy.

When I viewed this next one, I knew in a moment I needed to share this message. This is a nice-looking woman who must have been sitting on a cactus or had a burr in her saddle. I feel bad for this gal because, in my limited opinion, she has gotten very hurt and hasn't recovered yet and isn't ready to date anyone, not even Errol Flynn.

I am not interested!

These are real responses from real women on at least four dating sites. They're responding to my canned dating philosophy that I have designed and continue to update, modify, or improve, or it's a response to something they had had asked me or shared with me in on the various sites.

You might remember the following response from Beth. Do you think this woman really wants to meet a guy, or is looking for a pen pal?

Yes, I still have my business and intend to keep it as it's lucrative for me. I appreciate your honesty. I'm *not* moving from my historical home in Seguin or the Cabin Hideaway in the New Mexico mountains during the summer heat and

> humidity because of my asthma. I'm looking for a companion
> that is a good conversationalist and can travel who enjoys
> similar activities. Thanks for your honesty! Beth

She says she has a lucrative business and has a cabin hideaway in the mountains of New Mexico. She says she's looking for a good companion. Is she really? Or is she looking from someone to have good conversation with? She does say she likes to travel and wants to enjoy similar activities, but she is not moving! Who is going to move to the mountains? Rip Van Winkle?

As you read through these messages, I believe you will see that the gals are lonely, although not all. (I assume you could say this about a good many guys too.) This can be a good door-opener, but I would suggest this will start to breakdown fast, particularly if the distance is too far away to follow up with a dinner or lunch or other follow-up dates.

> Ok. Thanks for your response. Let me know whenever
> you're free. You sound nice. I am brand new on this site.
>
> > Betty

That one was kind of disappointing but maybe!

You likely will get messages from a number of gals who are out of your geographic area. As I've mentioned, you'll need to make a decision about this. Each dating site determines which of the women's profiles they show to you, based on your parameters, so you do have a degree of control by indicating the distance from your area you are willing to accept. But it often seems that the system disregards your range limits. This may be good or bad, depending on how willing you are to communicate with gals out of your range limit. I'd suggest that you determine this early. Of course, you can change your mind anytime to expand or reduce this. Remember, though, that the time you spend answering the gals who are beyond your range limits is time you could spend working on women who are within your range limit.

You'll also need to decide if you can afford the cost to participate on multiple sites—and this is totally up to your budget and how you believe it is going on one site.

There seem to be a good number of "normal" sites, but there also are some "hot spots"—and those hot spots will find you. At least three of them haunt me every day, and I didn't invite them in. I must admit I looked at two or more, and I got warnings from my security program that if I went any farther, I risked getting a virus. So a word to the wise before you cross this bridge: do not click on a site, especially the ones that for which you get a warning. In fact, just going halfway there may be too late; you could have a little problem on your hands.

Your search will be in your hands only. You might find very little good advice, and the even when you do, the advice that is good for you may not be worth anything to someone else. As an example, I have been told to go to church to meet women. I don't feel comfortable searching for a new love in church; I never met anyone in a church, and I attended for over thirty years. I don't feel comfortable looking for someone in a bar either. I've been told there are a lot of women in the grocery store and that I could meet someone there. Has this worked for you? I tried Walmart a few times. I've also gone to the small dance place in a bowling alley, and this worked once. One friend introduced me to someone once, about fifty years ago, and that worked. I also met a gal at the paint store down the street, about two miles from my house. I asked her out; she was married.

Still, if someone suggests a way that I can meet someone, I am going to try it because you never know.

When I worked at Lockheed in Sunnyvale, California, I am remembering meeting two gals at a bar not far from my first house; this was convenient. I also met someone suggested by a friend who gave me her phone number. I had never seen her or talked to her before, so it was a blind date with her. We were together for a number of months, although she got drunk on me on a number of occasions. I wanted to marry her, but it wasn't because I couldn't get a date. I had a number of girlfriends at that time. I owned a house and had a pretty fair job with a major company, but after her parents put off the wedding twice, I moved on.

I met the woman who eventually became my wife at a small dance bar in Cupertino, California, and a little over three months later, we were married. We had two kids together, and our marriage lasted about thirty years.

My third successful experience was someone I met through the dating tabloids in the early days. After about four months, we were married. I really loved this gal.

So this can happen almost anyplace. I believe that the dating site, with all its ups and downs and challenges, is as good or better than most other methods. If you think you've found the right one, be wise and use caution and smarts. Find the one that you think fits, and go for it. As I've said, you might decide to use more than one dating site for addition exposure. The greater your exposure, the better your chances are to find the one. Just like your car, you have to put a number of miles on it before you really know if you like it. You will not know by the number of doors, color, engine size, or price.

One more thing, when it gets down to the final evaluation, it is simply a numbers game and how you throw the dice.

To put it another way (and mix metaphors), if you shoot more baskets than the competing team, you should win, but you must have something worthwhile to sell—buggy whips are obsolete.

I recently spoke with a single friend who said he had met a woman, and she had offered to let him move into her remodeled garage. He wasn't too interested, though, because he discovered she didn't bathe. I said, "From my military background, I often shower twice a day, but a gal once told me that I smelled musty. I was taken aback, since I'd just had a shower, but I do use musk aftershave."

Or you may find a gal that you like, but she plays golf on Monday, is out with a girlfriend on Tuesday, plays cards on Thursdays, and has other responsibilities. She might not be willing to change her schedule, so you must decide: will this work for you?

CHAPTER 11

L **ET US TALK** about the information that dating sites use to match you with someone based on for personal compatibility:

1. Your astrological sign
2. Your height
3. Your gender
4. Your body type (slim, average, athletic, husky, etc.)
5. If you have (or want) children
6. Your education
7. If you consider yourself religious or spiritual and/or which religion you follow
8. Lifestyle (This is wide open but includes things like smoker or nonsmoker, social drinker or abstinent, homebody or party animal, etc.)

With some sites, this can leave a lot to be desired. Some suggest an open sentence to begin your story, such as, "I grew up in _____."

Some people go into detail; others just list the name of a town.

Photos vary as well. Some are so small you can't make out who is in the picture; others include too many extras—pets, flowers, group shots with several people, and so on. I prefer to have some idea of who I am talking to. I think most men are more interested in appearances. I would prefer Mary, for example, if she was a little nice-looking, not dumb as a stump and great-looking.

Some sites ask how you spend your leisure time. I believe this is important. For example, I don't fish, and I'm not terribly interested in going to professional sports activities, but a movie, the fair, or maybe a day trip are enjoyable for me. Compare what's most important to you and the women you are trying to meet.

Dating sites don't always ask for information about your occupation, but I believe this is an area that needs exploring. As they say, birds of a feather flock together, and it does seem that teachers hang with teachers, medical professionals hang with medical professionals, sales people hang with sales people, and so on. This isn't to say you can't go outside your own occupation, but having similar jobs gives you a commonality and something to talk about.

There's often space on the profile to write about the things that are important to you. Man, this is a biggy for me. I enjoy being by the water—ocean, lake, river, stream, pool. I'm not a big swimmer, but I like going to the beach and getting wet. My second wife didn't much like going in a pool. For us, this difference wasn't an issue, but you'll need to decide how you feel about having different ideas of what's important.

Game-Changers

A few weeks ago, I met a nice blonde on one of the sites, and we went out three times. In that third meeting, she said she liked to gamble. I related an experience I had in Nevada with my ex-wife. We were traveling from Wyoming and were just a few miles from the Nevada border, the last gambling spot on the freeway, when we came upon was a major auto accident. The cars on the freeway had come to a stop, so we took the first exit, which turned toward the casino. We often stopped there for a pit stop or maybe to eat, and we always enjoyed leaving our donation at the "Casino Rest Home of America for Broke Gamblers."

In fact, I would have been better off throwing the money out the window, but no, I went in. I had never played roulette before, but this evening I got started to play—and I was winning. I had to stop, though, because I started worrying about getting addicted and losing my winnings and the house payment. I mention this because I realized it would be good for me to know if my new girlfriend had a gambling addiction. Another game-changer for me would be tattoos, taking drugs, infidelity, or if the person was a sex offender.

One woman wrote that she enjoys the simple things in life. I wasn't sure what this meant. Does she like living in a tent in Alaska? She said she learns new things every day and broadens her horizons. This type of comment is very generic; what does this mean to you? How to bake an apple pie? Or is it studying economics or chemistry?

Another wrote that she likes to help those who need her. Well I need a gal/wife/girlfriend, and I am not sure I want to share her much. How much time is involved in her helping others and at what cost?

Some women indicate they want a man to be romantic, and this is good to know. I like girls, but some of us guys, as we get older, like hunting or fishing more than girls.

It's my opinion that the (now) five dating sites that I have been working with have little or no concern about appropriately matching women and men; in many cases, they're not even close. A large number of women post non-pictures or silhouettes, so the men who are looking are truly clueless. I have tried to be kind with suggesting that the gal forward a photo, and most of the time, they are willing to do so. It is sad, though, because for me, I would estimate that at least 15 percent of them are, I am sorry to say, less than appealing to me, which is a waste of time for both of us. I would suggest that maybe a composite be constructed by both individuals; that might help the site managers, and it also could give both parties an opportunity to find a favorable companion.

The appealing profile isn't all that's important. If you factor that another 10 to 15 percent are geographically inaccessible, it can be a total waste of both parties' time. You know by now that I have set a distance limit of fifty miles; some of us might be willing to go farther. I have found several women extremely physically desirable, and if there wasn't an issue about cost, I would break a leg trying to put something together. But for many of us, the economic situation would be next to impossible to manage. I think this should be a special section for those who would or could accommodate the additional cost.

As I've mentioned, at this point I have talked to or sent messages to well over four hundred women, sometimes more than once. The number may sound good, but I have been at this for nearly two years. You might remember that when I did this before meeting my second wife, I had far few women to interview, write to, or talk to, but I met more, dated more, and was rejected less and disappointed less.

There is another in gleaming issue, in my opinion, and this is race. Some men and women are interested in dating only within their own race or religion. I would check if the site takes the proper steps to allow the individuals to indicate this so that you don't have the embarrassment of telling a woman you're not looking for polar bears or kangaroos. I am a big boy, but I don't like to tell a gal I am not interested in her for either of these reasons.

Not too long ago, I met a very sweet seventy-seven-year-old blonde. We were talking about our different experiences, and she told me that she had met a guy on the site who lived in California. She was interested, so she agreed to fly from Texas to California to meet with him, and she did this several times. On a number of occasions, she said, when she got home, she discovered that one of her earrings was missing. She didn't think much about it the first time, but on the next visit, she also discovered an earring was missing. She asked the new friend if he had seen any earrings, and that was the end of the cross-country dating. How lucky for her, because we see this kind of thing on *Law and Order* all the time—they find a woman's photos all over the wall in the guy's apartment, and underwear or other personal items in the guy's drawers or closet. And the gal is found floating in the Pacific Ocean or maybe in a shallow grave. Not as many guys disappear this way, but it could happen to you. All I'm saying is this: be careful because the life you save could be your own.

A few weeks ago, I met a nice gal from near Grapevine, a very nice, quaint community near Dallas. We went to an upscale restaurant, and over dinner she told me that she was unhappy, with a guy she'd met recently. He was in a wheelchair with an oxygen tank, and she somehow learned that he was impotent too. She was surprised and disappointed, so this was not a good match of two people—not even close. I felt bad for the guy, but at the some point he should be matched with someone who isn't bothered by his physical limitations.

As I've mentioned, I have a lot of back pain at times, but sometimes I am friskier than a fifty-year-old. There are other times that I tell the gal I am with that when I was in the navy, I used to eat glass, spit bullets, and dance all night but not so much today. I don't jump as high as I used to or go down as low either. I have been talking to a nice gal who's a little younger than I am, but she's mentioned she needs her knees done, so there's a chance she wouldn't be running around that poop deck on the next cruise.

Another gal posted a nice picture—it's close enough that I can get a good idea of what she looks like. She has no children at home and says that she is active and "vocal." I'm not sure what this means. Will she yell at me when I am in the bedroom and she is in the kitchen? She's a retired schoolteacher looking for friendship and companionship. I would like the woman to say, "Yes, I would consider marriage," or "No, I don't want to get married again," or "I have been married twice, so this would be a major decision for me." This could be a major move for both you and the woman because of simple economics, family, and more. There are retirement income considerations. So each one of us has to be upfront and honest and communicate with someone with a lot of knowledge in this area.

Then we have the sexual relationship angle. Some are interested, some are not, some can, and some cannot. Some of us can be fixed or helped, and other can't. You need to work this out too and may need to see your physician. But have an open mind and consult someone with expertise in the area, not just your friends.

It's my opinion that if these sites were really interested in putting gals and guys together, they would spend more time in matching location. As I've mentioned, it's not impossible for a guy to date a gal who lives hundreds of miles away, but there is a whole lot of stuff that goes into an enterprise like that. Remember the time and financial investments involved.

With all the available technology, if a dating site tells people it's going to help them find a match, it needs to go a little farther, like work recognition, career backgrounds, childhood environments, and what individuals really want and are looking for. As an example, if you're really interested in marrying that the person you've met, wouldn't you want to know if you and she are on the same page? When we were in our twenties, we could look ahead to fifty more years here or more. Well wake up and smell the roses; many of us don't have this much time, so there's more of an urgency.

What do you want from your companion? If you don't marry her (or even if you do), are you interested in an intimate or platonic relationship? I am not looking for the latter any too soon. I may not be as fast and furious as I once was, but I don't want to give up trying. How long should you wait before you kiss or shower together? There is a real question. I like to shower every day with a woman. I call this recreational showering. Have you ever thought about it? Do you like to spend time necking? I really enjoy those long, passionate kisses. How long should they last? I really don't know, but I am in for a long ride.

As you know by now, when I met the woman who became my second wife, we moved in together a short time later, and we married about three months after we met. And we never looked back. We had a good arrangement—she oversaw all our finances, and this worked for me. She liked to be in control, but she didn't argue about my buying Cadillacs. We both willingly made compromises. I tried to subscribe to the philosophy, "Happy life, happy wife." And it worked for me.

Politics are important to some people, and it is interesting to know what political surroundings you are in. This can be more critical than religion. I talked to a gal a few months ago who clearly was a Democrat. In fact, her profile stated, "If you're not a Democrat, don't bother talking to me." I said that I really liked Harry Truman, the only one who did something that no other president has done. I told the gal that I also liked "Ike," another Republican president of the United States. But I also voted for Kennedy for president, a Democrat. Still, she dumped me before we could share any ideas. Another saying is, "Opposites attract," but that didn't seem to be the case with us.

A lot of important stuff about one another can bring you together or set you apart. I have been looking for a gal who would like to shoot at the range with me and might hunt wild pigs with me. If you were looking for such a gal, wouldn't it be nice to have this information?

CHAPTER 12

THE FOLLOWING ARE the best dating sites available if you are over fifty:

- Match
- eHarmony
- Our Time
- Christian Mingle
- Seniors Meet
- AARP Dating
- 50-Plus Club

The most effective dating sites are the following:

- Zoosk
- Match
- Our Time
- Elite Singles
- Black People Meet

The top four dating sites are:

- Zoosk
- Match
- Our Time
- Elite Singles

<u>The best over-forty dating site is Mature Singles.</u>

Elite Singles claims to have more than 100,000 new members per month. It's been suggested that the best site for finding true love is Singleandover50.com. To tell the truth, I have not used this site, but you might want to start here yourself. It's difficult to pick the "right" site, because it's not only picking the right site but the right time, saying and doing the right thing, and your potential mate doing the same thing. What is the probability of that happening? I don't have the foggiest idea, but I can assure you that without putting your hook in the lake, you are not going to catch a fish.

The best site for professionals may be virtualdatingassistants.com. This site uses special criteria to target the type of women (or men) you want to date as a professional. The downside is that the app is only available in a limited number of cities.

These sites can be seductive, but they also can be costly and, in my limited experience, also have short-term benefits, if that. Some could be a waste of your time and money, and some could, as I mentioned, give your computer a virus. But the choice is yours, and yes, more are available than those I've listed. It's more than to easy to find them.

The Best Free Dating Site

I don't have a lot of experience with free dating sites, so you'll need to do your own research. When I see anything advertised as "free," the red flag goes up. So I would suggest you go slow with "no-cost" dating sites. On the other hand, you haven't invested anything so if it doesn't work out for you, you haven't wasted your money.

Check out Coffee Meets Bagel, sign up, and instantly get connected with hundreds of local singles. You'll need to start by providing the basic information about yourself—sex, height, education. Do you smoke?

How often do you drink? What is your ethnicity, background, religion, salary? What are your interests? You can slant it one way or another. Interesting here that this research is not on Match.com. And of course it asks for the same personal information as you'll find on other sites.

I didn't expect much, and this is what I got—nothing visibly outstanding or over the top—so I suggest you take your own look and make your own evaluation. It's still my view that it's best to select more than one site, use them for a while, do a self-analysis, and either stay with it or try a new one.

I have not gone on every site, but I'd suggest that you do a search on your computer using the search words, "50+ Singles Dating" or something similar. This should allow you to meet singles in your area—or anywhere. You'll find most sites claim to have "millions of real users" if you're looking for romance. They may say you'll meet professional elites, marriage-minded college graduates, and more.

Safest Dating Sites for Singles Over Fifty

Just because it's "safe" to join an over-fifty dating site doesn't mean you should totally let your guard down. You will find numerous dating sites on the internet, but it may be difficult to find a trustworthy site. There are free sites and those that require a monthly membership fee. Unfortunately, more and more sites are becoming paid sites, but many seniors choose the paid sites anyway because they advertise more privacy options than the free sites. I can see this, but I am not sure how much better they are. With a little research, you should find dozens of sites, so take the time to find and read the reviews.

One of the top senior dating sites in the world is called Senior Match. You'll find countless members in the United States, the United Kingdom, Canada, Australia, and Europe. The site provides many features, such as senior dating ideas, fashion shows for seniors, online chat rooms, senior greeting cards, senior forums, senior blogs, privacy protection settings, email, and more. They claim to have a membership of over three million.

Other top sites are OlderOnlineDating.org, Millionaire Match (not a sugar daddy site, but a site for socializing with very successful, attractive people) and Older Women Dating, which for older women looking for younger men or younger men wanting to date an older woman. The site suggests that older woman are beautiful, confident and experienced. Yes, this is the "cougar" site.

If you're over seventy, you might find true love at Over70Dating. org (note that it's a dot-org, not a dot-com site). It provides a quick or advanced search, as well as advice, senior blogs, first-date ideas, email, and more. When I tried this site, I received the following replies from different women:

> I started on guitar at age 7. Always wanted a keyboard, my parents couldn't afford a piano. Stuck with the guitar until I got into high school and finally had a piano. I was in a band at age 11 and getting paid! After high school I bought an organ. Wasn't the kind I wanted but got hooked! At age 20 I was dating a young man my mom did not like. She offered me the down payment on a full Hammond B3 organ. He didn't stand a chance. Within three months I performed my first concert. Before age 21 I went pro, joined the musician's union and started playing professionally. Found that solo work was okay, but playing with drums, horns, guitar, was way more satisfying! I retired from playing in groups in 1976. Still play, still love it, but sold all my equipment before moving here. Am currently looking to replace what I had. Miss playing ... for my own ears! I traveled on the road with two different groups ... I think that's why I now love being home so much! I do not play church music, nor classical organ ... my taste in music rests in the blues field. One might say I have soul! Hope I did not bore you! Truly gave you the condensed version! Karen

The following is Jane in Oklahoma. In her photo she seems to be nice-looking. She says she's a good listener, and she has a very interesting family history, including some stories about Belle Starr and Geronimo and has an author in her background. If she was closer, I might meet her. But she's over 150 miles away, and I'm not romantically interested in meeting her. Although I won't suggest meeting, I hate to let her down by not continuing to communicate with her. I feel much younger than I am and have been told I look younger, too, but Jane is an old-looking eighty-two. She might be a friend if she was close, but I am not looking for a friend. I hate to tell her this. You may have to deal with these dilemmas, so be prepared.

Next there's Mable, who sent me a "smile." Then she wrote:

> 3:26 p.m.
> I've never taken a good picture in my life. I simply don't take good pictures but there is one on my profile.

> 10:52 p.m.
> I like your profile.

This is typical. She is a year younger than I am, but she just isn't that appealing to me. She's five foot four, a combination of Native American or Native Alaskan. She sounds good-hearted, and she said that she is looking for a relationship. I've seen so many women on dating sites say they are very much interested in having a relationship that it makes me laugh.

She likes to swim, fish, and camp out with nature. She would enjoy being romantic. Again, this is an example that the site management is more interested in just throwing several people up on the wall without really matching them. And here again, Mable lives in Kerrville, which is more than eighty miles from my location.

Here's another example: she sounds like a neat gal but she's new to the area. She's a music publisher and lives near me, but again, beauty is in the eye of the beholder. I am not attracted to her. And she has only a high school education

Choosing the Right Over-Fifty Dating Apps

A great many senior dating websites offer dating apps. It can be difficult and challenging to come up with the right app for you. Here are some factors that may help you decide:

1. How many singles over fifty are using the app?
    You need to think about how many people in your age range and area will use the app. This can be difficult to tell without

signing up, but there are specialized over-fifty dating sites and apps.

2. What are you looking for?
Many dating apps and sites are designed to match people who are not looking for serious relationships. This sometimes can be confusing, since my interest and the interest of the gals on some sites are not on the same page. But Match.com and OurTime are two options that are meant to find singles who are looking for long-term relationships.

3. Are you willing to pay for the service?
There are many free dating apps, but many of their features are locked to premium members. This can make it hard speak with or meet other singles unless you pay.

4. How many apps are you willing to sign up for and use?
The huge number of over-fifty dating apps can make it tempting to sign up for several. However, signing up for many online dating services can make it hard to keep track of who you are talking to. I was mixing up names, locations, the names of their dogs, and so forth.

If you continue to use these apps and sites, you will need to dig a little deeper to find one that fits your needs.

What do professionals tell us about these dating sites? Overall, the biggest advantage that dating sites have is that they offer large numbers of potential individuals to select from. That said, you still have the issues with distance and scamming. And here's the real kicker: we really don't know what we are looking for. If we don't know that, then we are in a lot of trouble from the get-go.

Experts may study this dilemma and develop some logarithms or related data, but what is an expert? Does my experience and background make me an expert? I have about eight years of college, a PhD, and I have done some research and conducted a research survey in Wyoming. From some of my experience on this subject—somewhat subjective—I have concluded that women and men don't know what they want and have a terrible time expressing it.

I have found a number of attractive women (some were not) with overwhelming personal, social, economic, and sexual qualities who extremely interested me, but at the same time, they told me, "I don't think we are a match." I never saw them, touched them, smelled them, held them in my arms, or had any kind of contact, so I have no idea how this conclusion can be made with no real evidence. I couldn't make this decision.

I feel that with my educational background, career, and travel, I am a little worldly. I don't do drugs, don't smoke, and don't really gamble. I have never killed anyone or beat up a woman. I have dated a few gals in my time, was engaged three times, and married for more than fifty-five years, total. This should suggest a solid background, If I was looking for a job or position, over ten years' experience would be pretty solid, but I have five times this. My limited conclusion here is that anyone who would take this position of saying we aren't a match has no idea what side of the street she is on or doesn't know what she wants and shouldn't be looking because she will make a big mistake. If you can say, for example, "Sam has bad breath," that can at least be evaluated. At least you have taken an assessment based on fact, good or bad.

So score of compatibility between us and the gals we are looking at has little benefit. I have said to women, "We have an extremely high compatibility score and should get together and talk." Not one lady has taken me up on this suggestion to meet based on this score. One, however, said she was interested in having sex with me. I found this somewhat surprising. Was she looking for a sugar daddy? Yes, I think so! The common denominator with these women—I am going to say seventy-year-olds and younger—is money.

Here is my comment on this: having some money is helpful, but I am looking for a look, body, face, shape, carriage, attitude, love, stuff in common, some sex, same politics, and maybe some of the same foods. And I hope the gal who will be my life likes my dogs.

I would suggest you make a list, remembering that you can compromise. As of this writing, the woman I am is a vegetarian. I will eat vegetables too, but I like Chinese food, American food, a good steak, fish, and ribs, and this works for her, and it works for me. I like a good cookie once in a while and a good soda too. She drinks water and tea.

As I've mentioned, I have a new gal, someone I met on one of the sites. I have a discussed some things with her early on and since then.

From the first day, you must tell the truth and have the courage of your convictions. But something came up that makes me wonder if this partnership will come crashing down. It was something that changed the direction of the flag. I don't know for sure; this is a day-by-day game.

I am spiritual, but my new girlfriend is not of my persuasion. She is a vegetarian, and I am not going to change my eating habits or ask her to change. We will find things to eat that we both like. We are both conservatives, but if she wasn't, I wouldn't try to change how she thinks. This would be, most likely, a game-changer too. I would have to find someone else instead. More than likely it isn't going to work. When the shine rubs off the new car, now you just have the car and no shine. I would like to keep the shine longer; you'll be much happier that way.

You may have more than one game-changer. For example, you may be passionate about your new wife not wanting to use your surname. Get this resolved before you are in divorce court. The cost today will be less than three months into your new marriage to this woman. If this is a game-changer for you now, you won't change later. My second wife wanted to keep her surname; everyone in the industry in which she worked knew her by that name. This is your choice—to say, "Sure, honey," or start a war you may not be able to win. You need to decide this now. Here is a piece of advice: "Happy life, happy wife." She also had her own credit cards, checking account, car, money, savings account—this worked for us. You will have to decide if it will work for you. Make this decision before you start dating this gal.

Where Is Your New Mate?

How many seniors over sixty-five are living in the United States? According to the US Administration of Aging, in 2011 there was an 18 percent increase from 2000. The Administration of Aging also reported that the number of Americans aged forty-five to sixty-four rose by 33 percent between 2000 and 2011. And many of these Americans are single, with 55 percent of women and 28 percent of men over sixty-five stating they were unmarried. The senior population has steadily increased with each passing year. Based on this information, I think we guys have the advantage.

The Upswing

Remarriage is on the upswing, although older adults remain more inclined to remarry than younger adults. Only 29 percent of previously married adults aged eighteen to twenty-four had remarried in 2013, compared with 67 percent of those aged fifty-five to sixty-four.

Among adults fifty-five and older, it has gone in the other direction. And in 2013, 67 percent of previously married adults, aged fifty-five to sixty-four, had remarried, up from 55 percent in 1960.

The reason may be that senior adults live longer. But lifespan and expectancies also has contributed to more divorces at older ages, as people realize they have more years to live and want a more fulfilling life in their longer life.

Who Is Most Eligible to Remarry?

It is not surprising that the most eligible are those adults whose first marriages ended in divorce or widowhood. Men are much more likely to seek out another partner to take the plunge with. In 2013, some 64 percent of men were eligible to marry, with 52 percent of women.

Some 29 percent of eligible men want to remarry and 36 percent are not sure, but in contrast, only 15 percent of previously married women want to remarry, 27 percent are not sure, and 54 percent have suggested that they didn't want to get remarry. This may be the issue with trying find the right gal. Women are dealing with personal conflicts because they don't really know themselves, and this is confusing to us guys. When you are selling your car, do you know how many miles it gets per gallon or at top speed or what size the tires are? And I am going to say you may not know yourself.

Among college graduates in 1960, only 40 percent of divorced or widowed women had remarried, compared with 75 percent of men, but by 2013, that had risen to 52 percent among women and had fallen to 67 percent among men. However, in less-educated groups, remarriage among women has stayed about the same but has declined a great deal among men. And it's interesting that those adults who are born in the United States are more likely to remarry than immigrants, although this is changing.

CHAPTER 13

MANY OF US seniors are looking for love and romance, but we face a number of obstacles. Here are a few issues that you may need to get through in your twilight years:

1. Older guys often develop a sense of inferiority because they are less virile compared to their younger selves. This may or may not be true, but I use to be able to run a hundred yards pretty fast. I just don't go there anymore. I'm a senior and deal with life from this point of view.

2. Older women often see themselves as unattractive because of society's worship of youth. I look at younger wife as more like being like a daughter; some are attractive, but I don't have an interest.

3. The older men often seek younger wives. It is common for an older man to start a new family, rather than pairing up with someone his own age, but this has never crossed my mind.

4. Women live eight years longer than men. This means that there are many lonely, widowed women whose prospects of finding another partner are slim. For example, in assisted living

communities, there is an average of seven women for each man. This might be true, but I have more to be concerned about.

5. Happiness is important at any age, but companionship plays a huge role in contributing to good quality of life and happiness as a senior citizen. If you or a loved one desires companionship after age sixty-five, you need to be proactive to rediscover the art of flirting, being confident, and finding a way to meet people. Still, no one is going to come knocking on your door. You have to put yourself out there.

6. Whether choosing a dating service, moving to an independent living community, or searching online, it's important to find your *joie de vivre* by seizing the day. After all, you are not getting any younger. If this is what you're looking for, the responsibility is yours.

What to Expect on Your First Senior Date

For most seniors, this maybe your first real date in a long time, so expect to be a little nervous. Being around other people may make you jittery, so try to stay cool. My former sales experience has helped me, as has my teaching experience and my having made several presentations. Just remember not to panic.

You may believe that you can't trust your first impressions, but this is not true. You don't need several dates to determine the viability of a new relationship. A man and woman can have feelings for each other from nearly the first time they meet. The most important thing here is to trust your instincts. Sometimes you can tell in moment if a person can light your fire.

Senior daters tend to be less impulsive—and this is a good thing. They have collected enough life experience to not fall for the first person they meet. However, what works for some doesn't work for others. It's possible to find a fulfilling relationship, as long as you're willing to wait for the right person to come along. I am going through this process, and it isn't simple.

Remember that it's important to think with your head and not your heart. You may believe that she is the right person, but force your mind to ask questions about key issues, like her financial situation. I have been down this road before, and my second wife and I set up a trust to protect each other. This is a place to start, if you get together with another individual.

Maintain eye contact, and make it clear that you expect the truth, not a sanitized version of it. After you have an important talk, if you still happy with your selection of potential partner, meet with a lawyer to set up a trust that will protect both your families. You'll also need to consider IRS and Social Security issues, as well as other related retirement matters in many cases.

Some say that opposites attract, but it seems that we usually want to find a person who has similar interests and ideas. People may resist the idea of seeking someone who's just like them because they fear that the individual with share their faults as well as their positive points. Someone who has a similar personality, however, and your tastes and temperament is more likely to be your soul mate than your evil twin.

At some point you should be able to move out of your brain and listen to your heart. At this point, it's time to trust it will keep you on the right path and that you are feelings are the ultimate truth.

If you've come this far, by now you realize that women are looking for honest men—those who tell the truth and do what they say. As I've mentioned, I bring flowers on every date. This isn't a requirement; I like to do it. But one thing I think about—so she will not take me for granted—is getting her something new, a slight change in the game. Instead of flowers, I'll bring my girlfriend something different tomorrow. If you wanted to be slick, you could follow the Twelve Days of Christmas, but this isn't just for special occasions. She is your special person, your girlfriend or lover. So how cool is this?

Are we missing something? It's important to realize that maintaining a positive and satisfying sex life helps us feel better, and this is true for both sexes. Women often find that what worked when they were younger doesn't necessary work for them now. Their sexual activity is more enjoyable and more stable as they have gotten older. About 13 percent of sexually active women today do not have a steady relationship.

So what about us guys? Older men generally can still enjoy a full and exciting sexual relationship; in fact, many are comfortable with their own bodies. Of course I don't run as fast as I used too, and I sometime criticize myself when I discover I'm a larger size than I was in my thirties. But we can be more confident about what our partners might enjoy, as we become more knowledgeable with age. My parts may not be as flexible as they once were, and I might have a little less stamina, and yes, libido does tend to decline with age. But that doesn't mean sex is no longer an option. And over half of people in their seventies are still having sex once a week or more. My doctor recently confirmed that men my age should expect to enjoy sex.

This isn't to say, however, that we don't have a few issues from time to time. Here are some delicate issues that we need to deal with:

There is a likelihood that we will develop an increase in ED with age. Still, this doesn't mean we want to sit and count the flies on the wall.

High blood pressure, heart disease, high cholesterol, vascular disease, diabetes, and prostate cancer are all issues we may face. But there is help for men, and it can make a difference. Your doctor can determine if certain medications can help you. There's more to sex than just intercourse, and you may experience greater satisfaction in knowing you are loved, wanted and cared for. There's more time to devote to caring and touching, and it can be more fun for all.

As I've mentioned, I take a gift nearly every time I meet my gal. Most women like this, and I do too. The gift says to them, "He's thinking about me!" And of course, this is what I want them to realize.

You can't draw a conclusion about women and dating from listening to your buddy, best friend, or the guy shooting his mouth off at the bar. Generally, women don't want a lot from a guy. They are looking for a few key qualities in a life partner, but these qualities may seem hard to find, even though every man can embody these qualities. They are not out of our reach, but most men lack at least one. You may conclude that no one is perfect, and no one has all these qualities, but this isn't necessarily true. Many men are sufficient enough in these areas to make a woman incredibly happy. That's all that matters, right?

- Be honest but not totally.

  A woman doesn't want a man to lie to her about important things, especially being an important part of his life, but she wants to know the things that are going on his life. She wants him to have trust in her. As far as she is concerned, they are one: his life is her life.

  If she asks you if she looks great, tell her she looks beautiful. The fact she gained fifteen pounds doesn't bother you; her new haircut makes her look even cuter. The only thing you should really lie about are shallow matters, such as appearance. We all look like crap sometimes, but she doesn't need to hear this from you.

- Understand her, so she doesn't need to explain herself.

  She wants you to know her, inside and out. Only then will you love her for being her. We all need confirmation that we're worth loving—the real us, not the people others perceive us to be. Some of us may not need such a confirmation of our value, but we all want it. But it's more than just that. To have someone understand you is having someone completely know you for the person you really are. There's no confusion; there's no misunderstanding or misconception. You know her for the person she really is, the real her that exists outside of herself. As long as she lives on, so do you.

- Let her know she matters to you.

  To be cared for means not to not be alone in this life. Most people are forced to care for themselves, and it's a lot more difficult than some people believe. Some of us are not in the right mind-set to care for ourselves. A woman wants you to be there for her when she needs someone, to share her burden. Make her life a little easier. She also will be there for you when no one else will. It's a good trade-off, don't you think

- Be strong, both mentally and physically.

  No woman wants a physical weakling; it's against her nature. That doesn't mean she won't settle for slightly less than Hercules, but you're a man, dammit. She wants to feel that when she's with you, you'll be intelligent and practice self-control, simply because you can. We're all still animals, and women will always be attracted to the stronger men. A woman doesn't want you to be strong for the sake of being strong; she wants you to be strong for her. It brings her pleasure, makes her feel safe, and turns her on. Do you honestly need more convincing?

- Show compassion.

    It shows her you're capable of loving.

- Provide financial and physical security.

    You don't need to be a millionaire. Most women will admire the traits required for turning oneself into a millionaire and not the money alone. The right woman will love you for you, but she does need you to make her feel secure. She wants to feel that you will protect her from physical harm. She wants to know that you'll keep her safe, healthy, and comfortable. Does she need you to keep her safe? To bring home the bread? No. But she'd like you to be capable of it, even if her salary is bigger than yours. She'll have your back too, so you can rest easier as well.

- Give her blind loyalty; let her know she's the only woman you have eyes for.

    We all have big egos, men and women alike. We want to feel special. We want to feel unique and better than the rest. We're competitive by nature, and there is no getting around it. Women want a man who sees the world in her—her and only her.

    She knows she's not the most beautiful or smartest woman in the world, but she doesn't need to be; she's not delusional. She just wants you to think—to know—that she's the most beautiful, best woman in the world for you. She needs you to think she is the best thing that ever happened to you. She wants to be the best, and she wants a man who will allow her that title.

CHAPTER 14

ONCE YOU'VE MET someone, how can you tell if she cares about you? We are all in the same boat here, not only us guys but even the gals—the woman you are talking to or dating also needs to know that you really care. She'll often be on your mind. And you can show this by remembering her birthday, family, the things she likes to do. If she cares about you, you'll likely see the following:

- You will be on her mind.

    In recent conversations with my new gal, she mentioned getting her nails done, and she called me up in the process of managing one of our upcoming dates. She remembered that I also like getting my nails done, and she wanted to know if it was OK to set an appointment for me at the same time as hers, so we could get our nails done together.

- She wants to know about your days.

    A woman who cares about you wants to know every detail about your days. She wants to know what you are doing, your activities, and your events.

- Your health is important to her.

  If she care about you, she also will care about your health. She might be a finicky gal who forbids you to eat something or suggests you eat something else. She will act like your attendant. Then, if you catch cold, she will be your nurse. She will be at your side in your weak days.

- Your future is her concern.

  A woman who cares for her man will be concerned about her man's future. She will give advice like a fortune teller and ponder everything for your future. She will be your supporter.

- Your family is her heart.

  If you have a gal who cares about your family, it is a sign that she also cares about you. A caring woman will also care for your family. She will be interested in your little brother, mom, father, or other family members. Moreover, she will also remember your pets and will talk and care for your dog, cats, and so forth.

  Your happiness is one of her goals.

  Caring is sharing. If the women cares about you, she will feel your sorrows; in your sadness, she will try to make you happier. She will try to entertain you because your happiness is her goal. Your happiness is her happiness.

- Your well-being is her lullaby.

  Someone who cares about you will be peaceful when she knows you have good health and happiness. She will not sleep if she finds you in a bad condition, unhealthy, or sad. Your well-being is her lullaby. She will be fine at night after she knows you are OK.

- Your personal growth is her spirit.

  If you feel like giving up because you don't achieve your goals, she will come to your aid. She will be concerned about your personal growth and get more involved to help you achieve personal growth. The achievements in your life is her spirit and her achievement.

- She makes time.

   She is a hard worker, but she has still time for you. This is a sign she cares. A girl who cares about you will always try to make time for you. She will write your time together in her schedule.

- She's ready to listen.

   She will always listen to your stories. You can make a list of women and eliminate them until you find one who is always ready to listen to your stories. I have one of those who cares about hearing my stories. She's a good listener.

- She replies to your messages quickly.

   You will not have to wait, if she cares about you. She will reply to your message quickly (if she is free). But if she's busy, she will put you on her priority list and reply to you as quickly as she can.

- She will congratulate you on special days.

   You may wonder how she can remember each of your special days or events, but if she cares, she will not miss your special events.

- She will never embarrass you.

   A woman who cares about you won't make fun of you in public and never will share embarrassing information about you. She won't make you the butt of a joke. She enjoys her time with you. She cares about your self-esteem.

- She remembers your outfit.

   She will remember what you were wearing last night and your everyday outfit when you meet her. You are always in her sight.

- She knows your likes or dislikes.

   She will discover what you like and don't like, and she will give you what you want. She will avoid what you don't like. She loves to make you happy.

- She'll look at you affectionately.

    There could be a distinction between caring and love. But caring is the one part of love. If she cares about you, she will love you and look at you with affection.

- She'll apologize.

    Misunderstandings are common, but if she cares about you, she will apologize if she's in the wrong.

- She'll let you know why she's angry with you.

    Women will get angry at you if you do wrong or do something dangerous for your life; it is a sign of caring. She cares about your condition. And you'll know that she is not only falling in love with you, but she is also showing that she cares. Please keep her, and make her always feel special.

- She makes eye contact.

    Do you catch her eyes on you? Then she smiles; it is a sign if you are for her. She loves eye contact with you; she wants to show her desire for you.

- She plans to hang out alone with you.

    She does not like to hang out with your group of friends, but she invites you to spend Saturday night with her.

- She plans exclusive time.

    A women who sees you as a special will leave her phone number and make you as exclusive as she can. She will turn off the phone and enjoy your time with her. You are too special for her to let go. Together time with you is her exclusive time.

- She sees you as passionate.

    A woman who see you as passionate generally wants you more; she wants to have a relationship with you. She always smiles at you, loves to talk with you, is happy for your success, and wants to be involved in your activities.

- She smiles at you.

    If you she smiles at you for no reason, it's because you are a reason for her smile. She loves to smile when you are looking at her. She gets a happy feeling when you give her your eye contact.

- She compliments you.

    If you have a big achievement or even a small one, she will compliment you. You are a valuable person for her.

- Your activities are important.

    She will love everything about you, including the detailed information about your activities. She wants to know about them; it is important for her.

- She chooses you over time with the girls.

    Yes, this is a classic sign. She will avoid her friends to be closer to you.

- She's touchy-feely.

    Your gal will love to be close to you and love to be around you. Moreover, she will love to touch you. It's a sign if you are her lovey. Physical contact is common in special relationship.

- She will dressing up.

    She'll try to show herself in a better or a special appearance. She will dress up because she wants you in a relationship and loves you this much.

- There will be no other guy.

    She will avoid being close with another guy. She will keep you as the closest person. She doesn't want to be in a relationship with any other guy.

- She avoids mentioning another guy.

    She will try to avoid mentioning other guys in front of you if she sees you as her everything. She will consider you as her man.

Having a special relationship with a woman is not easy, but if you use the information above, it can be easier for you. You can get a better handle on the situation and make your love story really happen.

ABOUT THE AUTHOR

D R. FERRIS E. (Gene) Merhish is a college, adult education, and high school instructor, with over eighteen years of teaching experience. He was trained in business education, distributive education, and marketing and sales, with experience as an entrepreneur. He was recognized as a business education consultant for the state of California.

Several years ago he operated one of the most advanced programs in teaching or retail merchandising in the western United States. He also has been a department chair in a Southern California high school, where he has also taught computer technology and wrote a training workbook for the course.

In addition, Dr. Merhish has over twenty-six years of business and marketing experience with such firms as Proctor & Gamble, Gardner-Denver, and Harnischfeger Corporation and has created and operated at least two entrepreneurial companies. He has served as a business and marketing (adjunct) instructor for Ivy University in Alhambra, Riverside Community College, Chaffey Community College in Rancho Cucamonga, and others.

He worked in consort with the China Training Center for Senior Civil Servants, Ministry of Personnel, and the People's Republic of China, and Orange County Juvenile Hall, Job Corps, Furthermore,

Dr. Merhish works with small businesses as a marketing and sales consultant.

His first book was *7,001 Resumes*, now in its second edition. *The Dating Game* is Dr. Merhish's fourth book and is based on direct research and experience as a widower seeking a new companion with whom to move forward in the sunset of his life, sharing love and happiness with his new companion.

Printed in the United States
By Bookmasters